W9-BSZ-357

OECD
ECONOMIC
SURVEYS

1993-1994

SPAIN

ORGANISATION FOR ECONOMIC CO-OPERATION AND DEVELOPMENT

ORGANISATION FOR ECONOMIC CO-OPERATION AND DEVELOPMENT

Pursuant to Article 1 of the Convention signed in Paris on 14th December 1960, and which came into force on 30th September 1961, the Organisation for Economic Co-operation and Development (OECD) shall promote policies designed:

- to achieve the highest sustainable economic growth and employment and a rising standard of living in Member countries, while maintaining financial stability, and thus to contribute to the development of the world economy;
- to contribute to sound economic expansion in Member as well as non-member countries in the process of economic development; and
- to contribute to the expansion of world trade on a multilateral, non-discriminatory basis in accordance with international obligations.

The original Member countries of the OECD are Austria, Belgium, Canada, Denmark, France, Germany, Greece, Iceland, Ireland, Italy, Luxembourg, the Netherlands, Norway, Portugal, Spain, Sweden, Switzerland, Turkey, the United Kingdom and the United States. The following countries became Members subsequently through accession at the dates indicated hereafter: Japan (28th April 1964), Finland (28th January 1969), Australia (7th June 1971), New Zealand (29th May 1973) and Mexico (18th May 1994). The Commission of the European Communities takes part in the work of the OECD (Article 13 of the OECD Convention).

3 2280 00497 9621

Publié également en français.

© OECD 1994
Applications for permission to reproduce or translate
all or part of this publication should be made to:
Head of Publications Service, OECD
2, rue André-Pascal, 75775 PARIS CEDEX 16, France

Table of contents

3

Tables

Diagrams

5

BASIC STATISTICS OF SPAIN

THE LAND

Area (thousand sq. km)	504.8	Major cities, 1991 census (thousand inhabitants):	
Agricultural area (thousand sq. km)	203.2	Madrid	3 010
		Barcelona	1 644
		Valencia	753
		Seville	683

THE PEOPLE

Population, 1992 (thousands)	39 085	Civilian employment, 1992 (thousands)	12 366
Number of inhabitants per sq. km	77	Employment by sector, per cent of total:	
Net natural increase, 1991 (thousands)	60	Agriculture	10.1
Net migration, 1991 (thousands)	2	Industry	22.7
		Construction	9.7
		Services	57.5

PRODUCTION
(1992)

Gross domestic product		GDP at factor cost by origin, per cent	
(GDP, billion pesetas)	58 852	of total:	
GDP per head (US$)	14 704	Agriculture	4.3
Gross fixed investment:		Industry	18.8
per cent of GDP	21.9	Construction	9.1
per head (US$)	3 214	Services	63.4

THE GENERAL GOVERNMENT
(1992)

Public consumption, per cent of GDP	16.8	Government revenue, per cent of GDP	40.1
Fixed investment, per cent of gross		General government deficit,	
fixed capital formation	19.7	per cent of GDP	4.5

FOREIGN TRADE
(1992)

Exports of goods and services:		Imports of goods and services:	
billion US$	101.1	billion US $	117.5
per cent of GDP	17.6	per cent of GDP	20.5
Exports by commodity group as a per cent		Imports by commodity group as a per cent	
of total, customs basis:		of total, customs basis:	
Foodstuffs	12.7	Foodstuffs	7.6
Other consumer goods	28.8	Other consumer goods	20.3
Fuels and lubricants	2.5	Fuels and lubricants	9.9
Other intermediate goods	41.9	Other intermediate goods	44.3
Capital goods	14.0	Capital goods	17.9

THE CURRENCY

Monetary unit: Peseta		Currency units per US$,	
		average of daily figures:	
		Year 1993	127.2
		March 1994	138.8

Note: An international comparison of certain basic statistics is given in an annex table.

This Survey is based on the Secretariat's study prepared for the annual review of Spain by the Economic and Development Review Committee on 8th April 1994.

•

After revisions in the light of discussions during the review, final approval of the Survey for publication was given by the Committee on 19th May 1994.

•

The previous Survey of Spain was issued in April 1993.

Introduction

After five years of fast GDP growth averaging 4¾ per cent per year, the Spanish economy has been in a period of adjustment since 1991. Following the trend in OECD Europe, Spain went into recession in mid-1992, and in 1993 GDP fell by 1 per cent, the sharpest decline in thirty years. At the beginning of the downturn investment was the main depressive demand component, but in 1993 the negative trend was accentuated by the change in the saving behaviour of households in the face of the steep rise in unemployment, leading to a sizeable fall in private consumption in 1993. However, underpinned by the depreciation of the peseta, the surge in net export volumes moderated the fall in output. The widening output gap and continuing high wage rises reinforced labour dishoarding, pushing the unemployment rate to almost 24 per cent at the end of 1993. The growing slack damped domestic inflationary pressures, so that, despite the depreciation of the peseta, consumer price inflation fell to 5 per cent at the turn of 1993. The adjustment in the external sector was also quite large; in particular the current balance of payments deficit shrank to ¾ per cent of GDP in 1993, one fourth of the average level of the previous three years.

In line with the immediate anti-inflation goals and also in order to meet the Maastricht Treaty's fiscal criteria, the authorities had designed a fairly restrictive policy stance for 1993. However, partly because of the cyclical weakening in activity, considerable fiscal slippage occurred and the general government deficit reached 7¼ per cent of GDP. Preoccupied by speculation against the peseta, the authorities kept interest rates at very high levels in the first five months of 1993. Monetary policy eased markedly in the second half of the year, even though monetary conditions were still tight overall. In 1994 the policy mix is better balanced, fiscal policy having been tightened and monetary conditions eased further. Moreover, the Government has presented important structural reforms, notably a comprehensive labour market reform. The improved macroeconomic policy setting and the favourable effects of structural reforms are expected to buoy business confidence and facilitate the upturn.

According to OECD projections, the recovery in activity will be fairly moderate in 1994, with a GDP growth slightly above 1 per cent. It is only in 1995 that GDP growth seems likely to be sufficiently strong to lead to net employment creation, so that after peaking at 25 per cent the unemployment rate may start declining in the course of 1995. After a slight pause in the early part of 1994, disinflation is expected to resume in the second half of the year, with 12-month consumer price inflation falling to $3^1/_2$-4 per cent by the end of the year. Structural reforms are expected to reinforce disinflation in 1995. The current balance of payments deficit is projected to shrink further in 1994.

Part I of the draft Survey discusses economic developments in 1993 and the immediate causes behind the marked fall in domestic demand. Macroeconomic policies, in particular the causes of the large fiscal slippage in 1993 and the measures to rein in the budget deficit in 1994, as well as structural policies, are examined in Part II. The OECD projections for 1994 and 1995 and the assumptions behind them are presented in Part III. With a 24 per cent unemployment rate, labour market disfunctioning is clearly the main issue in Spain today. Part IV analyses labour market developments since 1985, focusing on the factors responsible for high unemployment and policies conducive to restoring strong employment growth.

I. Economic developments in 1993

After five years of rapid expansion, GDP growth slowed markedly in 1991, before starting to decline in mid-1992, roughly at the same time as in OECD Europe. Turbulence in foreign exchange markets and pressure on the peseta led to a marked tightening in monetary policy stance in the summer of 1992, at the time that domestic demand started to contract, thereby reinforcing the downward trend in activity. Interest rates were very high from mid-1992 to mid-1993, but, influenced by the deterioration in fundamentals, the attacks against the peseta were so strong that the peseta was devalued three times over this period. Spain also suffered from financial stress, but less than many OECD countries. Private investment was the main contractionary force. In addition private consumption, which usually smooths out the downturns, declined, so that the fall in domestic demand reached 3½ per cent in 1993. At the same time, spurred by the devaluation effects, there was a sizeable shift of resources to the external sector. The consequent rise in net exports partly offset the weakness in the domestic market, but the fall of GDP was much sharper than the average in OECD Europe. GDP declined markedly in the first half of 1993 and broadly stabilised in the second half year. Weak activity set the stage for a continuing fall in employment during the second half of 1993 (though at a sharply slower rate than before), and contributed to easing inflationary pressures.

Falling domestic demand

Apart from the decline in the wage bill in real terms (due to the fall in employment), all other household income components continued to grow in real terms in 1993 (Table 1). This, coupled with a decline in the tax burden, led to a further small increase in real household disposable income in 1993. However, private consumption declined by as much as 2¼ per cent, due to a marked

11

Table 1. **Demand and output**

Per cent change, annual rate

	GDP shares 1992	$\frac{1990}{1986}$	1991	1992	1993 [1]
Private consumption	63.2	5.0	2.9	2.1	-2.3
Government consumption	16.8	6.7	5.4	3.8	1.6
Gross fixed investment	21.9	12.1	1.7	-3.9	-10.3
Final domestic demand	101.8	6.8	3.0	0.9	-3.5
Total domestic demand	102.8	6.9	2.8	1.1	-3.6
Exports of goods and services	17.6	4.4	7.9	6.7	8.8
Imports of goods and services	20.4	14.8	9.0	6.6	-3.2
Foreign balance [2]	-2.8	-0.1	-0.8	-0.4	2.9
GDP at constant prices		4.8	2.2	0.8	-1.0
GDP at current prices	100.0	11.6	9.4	7.4	3.4
Memorandum items:					
Gross fixed investment					
Private sector [3]	17.5	11.3	1.1	-2.5	-12.9
General government	4.3	15.5	4.3	-9.2	0.4
Real household disposable income		4.6	4.0	0.2	0.0
Household saving ratio, net (per cent)		5.4	6.9	5.2	7.4

1. OECD projections.
2. Contribution to growth of GDP.
3. Including companies under state control.
Source: Data submitted by national authorities and OECD estimates.

increase in the net saving rate to 7½ per cent, compared with an average of 5¼ per cent in the preceding ten years. This increase reflects higher precautionary savings on account of the rise in unemployment and the bleak outlook. In addition, between 1987 and 1991 households borrowed heavily to finance sizeable purchases of consumer durables (including cars) and new houses, resulting in a rise of the ratio of financial liabilities to disposable income from 0.73 in 1986 to 0.86 in 1990-92, with debt servicing costs growing even faster since the mid-1980s.[1] The desire to reduce their net debt position was reinforced by negative wealth effects resulting from the fall in real estate and share prices in real terms from the high levels of the early 1990s.

The growth in government consumption slowed to 1½ per cent, by far the lowest rate since 1969. After falling by 9 per cent in 1992, government fixed investment recovered slightly in 1993, which is in line with the Government's goal to maintain investment at a high level in order to improve the infrastructure and, at this phase of the business cycle, also to support activity. This is reflected in an almost 100 per cent rise in the central government's procurement bids and in some 20 per cent by regional governments and local authorities combined in 1993. The support provided by the authorities, including interest rate subsidies under the "Housing Plan, 1992-95", also led to a further rise in investment in *social housing* in 1993. However, this was more than offset by the depressive impact on private residential construction of high interest rates, a fall in house prices (particularly in prices of secondary houses) and more importantly by uncertain employment prospects.[2] As a result, residential investment continued to decline, making for a cumulative fall of 14 per cent in the three years to 1993.

After reaching very high levels in 1991-92 (15¾ per cent of GDP), business investment plummeted in 1993, but it was still over 10 per cent higher than the average level of the second half of the 1980s (Diagram 1). This fall is explained by a combination of factors: high interest rates, falling sales and the uncertain outlook, and cash flow difficulties resulting from the marked compression in net profit rates (in relation to equity) from nearly 10 per cent at the end of the 1980s to almost zero in 1992. However, small and medium-size firms, continued to have relatively high net profit rates in 1992 (7 and 2 per cent respectively), while large-size firms (on account of state firms) recorded losses for the first time in eight years.[3] Moreover, apart from industry, with a net loss rate of 10 per cent, all other sectors continued to show profits in 1992. The fall in investment in 1993 seems to have particularly affected transportation equipment and buildings.

The marked decline in private sector domestic final expenditure in 1993 was reinforced by a markedly lower rate of inventory accumulation. However, the latter was essentially a correction from the exceptionally strong, largely involuntary stockbuilding in 1992. Total domestic demand fell by 3½ per cent in 1993, which is by far the largest drop for over 30 years (the previous one was 2 per cent in 1981). A positive factor in 1993 was the marked rise in net exports. Overall, the decline of GDP was limited to 1 per cent in 1993 as a whole. With GDP falling by 2 per cent at an annual rate, between mid and end-1992, there was a significant negative "carry-over" at the start of 1993. During the first half of 1993, GDP continued its downward trend at a slower pace, and broadly stabilised during the second half at the low second-quarter level.

Diagram 1. **INVESTMENT INDICATORS**[1]

1990 = 100, seasonally adjusted

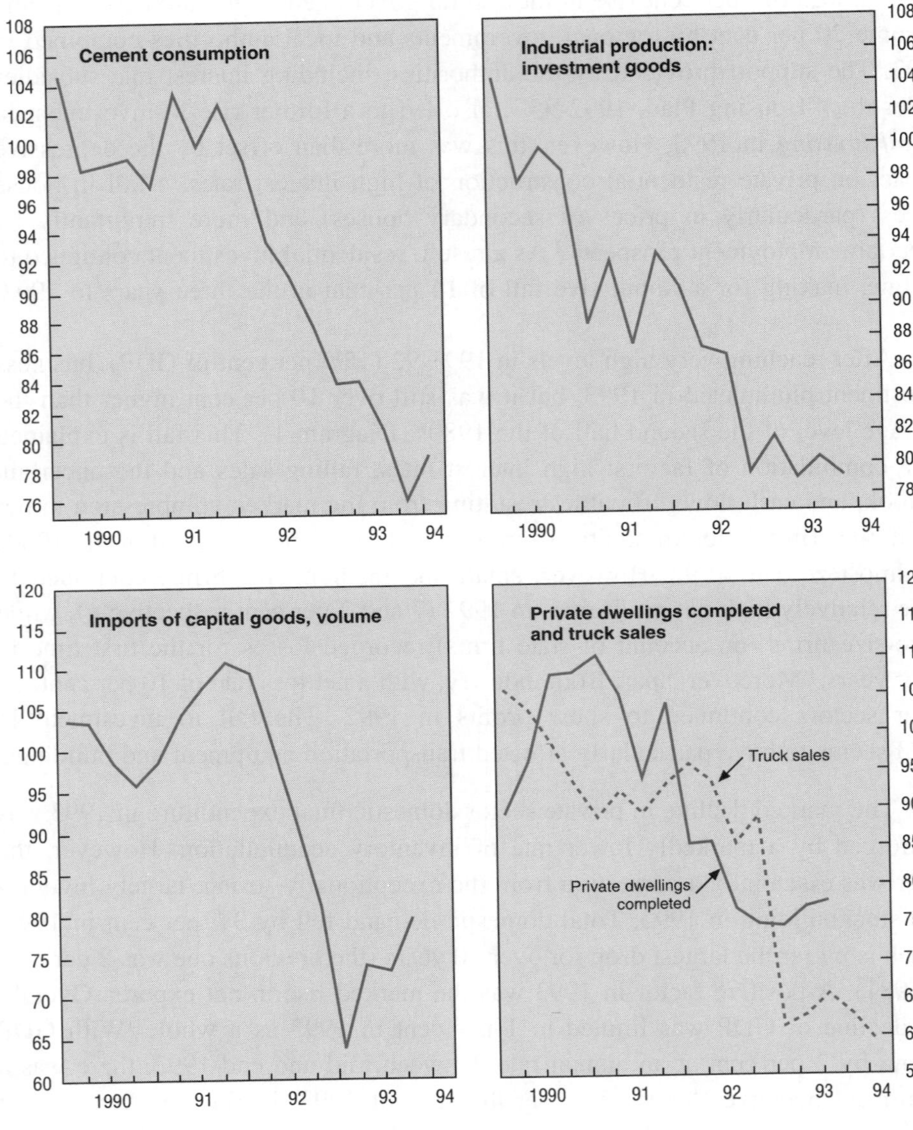

Cement consumption
Industrial production: investment goods
Imports of capital goods, volume
Private dwellings completed and truck sales
Truck sales
Private dwellings completed
1990
91
92
93
94

1. Quarterly averages of monthly data.

Source: Ministry of Economy and Finance and other national sources.

Labour shake-out continues

Job losses exceeded all previous records. The labour shake-out was particularly strong during the second half of 1992, when the decline in total employment reached a 5 per cent annual rate. Despite a slowdown in job destruction during 1993, employment fell by 4.3 per cent for the year as a whole and 7 per cent cumulatively between end-1990 and end-1993 (Table 2). Full-time employment fell even faster than total employment in 1993. The rates of decline in dependent and non-dependent employment were broadly similar. Moreover, contrary to the past upward trend, non-dependent non-farm employment declined as the generalised slack reduced the scope for new entrepreneurial initiatives.

Table 2. **Labour market trends**

	1989	1990	1991	1992	1993	1993 Q4
	Per cent change over previous year					
Total labour force	1.3	1.4	0.4	0.5	1.1	1.4
Total employment	4.1	2.6	0.2	−1.9	−4.3	−3.5
Non-farm employment	5.7	4.1	1.5	−1.3	−4.3	−3.4
Employees	6.2	4.4	1.1	−3.2	−4.3	−3.4
Non-farm employees	7.4	4.9	1.2	−2.6	−4.2	−3.4
Labour productivity, total [1]	0.6	1.0	2.0	2.8	3.4	
Business sector, non-farm	−0.1	−0.4	1.1	2.7	3.5	
of which:						
Manufacturing industry	0.0	−0.9	2.5	0.8	7.2	
	Per cent					
Participation rate [2]	59.5	60.0	60.0	60.0	60.3	60.7
Employment rate [2]	49.1	50.2	50.1	48.9	46.5	46.1
Unemployment rate [3]	16.9	15.9	16.0	18.1	22.4	23.4
Recipients of unemployment benefits [4]	49.4	59.0	69.1	80.4	82.7	78.4
	Thousands					
Placements	4 327	5 159	5 066	4 708	4 884	
Dismissals [5]	216	334	317	342	558	

1. On the basis of GDP at factor cost. Figures for 1993 are OECD estimates for 1993 as a whole.
2. As a percentage of working-age population.
3. Standardised unemployment rate. Seasonally adjusted for Q4 1993.
4. As a per cent of registered unemployment, excluding the farm sector and first time job seekers.
5. Including workers temporarily laid-off.
Source: National Institute of Statistics, Ministry of Economy and Finance, and OECD estimates.

In addition to the delayed response to the labour overhang that had developed up until 1991, the sharp labour adjustment in 1993 is also explained by wage rigidity. Faced with continuing strong real and nominal wage growth, as analyzed in Part IV, employment losses were particularly important in sectors subject to foreign competition (*e.g.* 10 per cent in manufacturing), especially in branches where labour costs weigh heavily.[4] The effort to economise on the wage bill is also underlined by the increasing capital intensity of business investment, which contributed to the apparent decline in capital productivity combined with a marked rise in the apparent labour productivity in 1993. In the protected sectors, job losses were relatively small; in the services sector, employment fell by only some 1½ per cent.

1993 witnessed an important change in public sector employment behaviour. First, after remaining broadly stable (allowing for changes due to privatisation) since 1985, employment in public enterprises fell by almost 10 per cent in 1993. This decline was concentrated on tradeable sectors as a result of long-delayed restructuring plans in mining, iron and steel and shipyards. Second, after rising by 4¾ per cent yearly between 1985 and 1992, employment in the general government decreased in 1993. In particular, reflecting budget constraints, central government employment (excluding the transfer of personnel to regional governments) seems to have fallen by 2 per cent, compared with a rising trend in the past.

The decline in employment coupled with an acceleration in labour force growth (see Part IV) led to a marked rise in the rate of unemployment to almost 24 per cent at the end of 1993, 4 percentage points up in one year. The rise in unemployment affected particularly young people (aged 16-24), so that one out of two was unemployed at the end of 1993. In addition to the fact that new entrants into the labour market suffer most in periods of slack, the termination in 1992 of subsidies for training young people reinforced the upward unemployment trend of this age group. The strong impact on unemployment of the rapid labour force growth is illustrated by the smaller change in the employment rate (those employed as a per cent of working age population aged 16-64) to 46 per cent at the end of 1993 from 48 per cent at the end of 1992 and 45 per cent in 1985. It is also worth noting that whereas the employment rate for prime-aged males fell by 3 percentage points between end-1992 and end-1993, that of prime-aged females was broadly stationary. In total, unemployment figures, boosted by the steep rise in the participation rate (0.6 percentage points), exaggerate the deterioration in overall labour market conditions in the course of 1993.

Slowly subsiding inflation

Despite the marked increase in unemployment, business sector wages grew in 1993 at the high rate of 6½ per cent (national accounts basis), the same as in 1992. Including an increase in social security contributions, the increase in compensation per employee was about 7½ per cent (Table 3). However, these rates include the carry-over from 1992, sizeable increases under previous multi-annual wage settlements as well as the triggering of indexation clauses and, therefore, mask to some extent the wage disinflation that was occurring in the course of 1993. New settlements towards the end of 1993 provided for basic wage rises of 5¾ per cent, 1½ percentage points below the end-1992 levels. However multi-annual agreements, which accounted for one-quarter of all settlements in 1990 have been on the rise since, and in 1993 they accounted for 37 per cent of new wage settlements. The rise of multi-annual agreements will hamper future wage flexibility,[5] especially in many public sector enterprises which signed a 3-year wage agreement (1993-95) in 1993.

Table 3. **Wages and labour costs**

Per cent change, annual rate

	1990	1991	1992	1993
Collective wage agreements	8.1	7.9	7.2	5.6
Including impact of previous year's indexation clause	9.2	8.1	7.3	5.7
Basic hourly pay	9.1	9.1	8.4	7.0
Average earnings in industry	8.4	8.9	8.0	6.5
Compensation per employee [1]	8.2	8.5	8.9	7.4
Unit labour costs, business sector (non-farm)	8.7	7.3	6.0	3.8
of which:				
Manufacturing	8.9	5.7	7.6	0.3

1. Private sector.
Source: Ministry of Economy and Finance, *Síntesis Mensual de Indicadores Económicos,* Bank of Spain, *Boletín Estadístico* and OECD estimates.

Despite the high and broadly stable wage rises, non-farm business sector unit labour cost growth slowed to 3¾ per cent in 1993 from 6 per cent in 1992, and in manufacturing to less than ½ per cent from 7½ per cent. This is due to rapid recession-induced productivity advances in 1993. Non-farm business sector productivity growth reached 3½ per cent, up from 2¾ per cent in 1992 and ½ per cent between 1985 and 1991; and 7¼ per cent in manufacturing compared with ¾ per cent in 1992 and 1½ per cent between 1985 and 1991. The lower indirect tax burden, reflecting delays in paying VAT and probably greater tax fraud (especially on imports) also eased the pressure for price rises in many sectors. Likewise, profits in non-financial sectors seem to also have absorbed part of the cost increases. In particular, faced with sluggish demand, importers and more generally domestic traders seem to have passed through only part of the rise in import and ex-factory prices to consumers. This is borne out by the deceleration through 1993 in the 12-month consumer price rise of industrial (non-energy) goods, compared with a steepening in wholesale (industrial) price rises of consumer goods over the same period. In total, the increase in the GDP price deflator fell to 4½ per cent in 1993, 2 percentage points less than in 1992 and the lowest rate since the 1960s (Table 4).

The marked weakening in domestic sources of inflation was largely offset by the turn-around from a fall in goods' import prices by 1 per cent yearly (national accounts basis) between 1989 and 1992 to an officially estimated increase of 7 per cent in 1993.[6] This is considerably less than the depreciation of the peseta (which amounted to 12 per cent in effective terms in 1993 and 18 per cent cumulatively between end-1991 and end-1993), and indicates cuts in the foreign suppliers' profit margins in order to maintain production in the face of weakening demand.

Consumer-price inflation fell from about 6 per cent in 1991 and 1992 to 4½ per cent in 1993 as a whole, but, because of an abrupt rise in the volatile food component towards the end of 1993, the 12-month increase in consumer prices rose to 5 per cent in December 1993. Apart from food prices, all other components of the consumer price index recorded a considerably slower increase during 1993 than in the previous year. Non-food and non-energy consumer price inflation fell from a relatively stable rate of 6½-7 per cent in the period 1987-92 to 5 per cent at the end of 1993.[7] The fall in inflation in services – from almost 9 per cent in 1991 and 1992 to 6.8 per cent in December 1993 – is an even more

Table 4. **Prices**

Per cent change over previous year

	1991	1992	Dec. 1992	1993	Dec. 1993	March 1994
Consumer prices	5.9	5.9	5.3	4.6	4.9	5.0
Food	3.5	3.7	1.3	1.1	4.4	5.5
Energy	7.6	6.7	10.1	7.5	6.4	5.1
Other industrial goods [1]	4.9	4.5	5.1	4.3	3.3	3.7
Services [1]	8.7	8.9	8.6	7.7	6.8	5.9
Non-food and non-energy [1]	7.2	7.1	7.2	6.0	5.0	4.8
Industrial prices	1.5	1.4	1.6	2.4	3.3	4.1
Consumer goods	3.5	2.9	2.2	3.4	4.5	5.0
Capital goods	3.5	2.3	1.9	1.3	1.2	1.3
Intermediate goods	-0.7	-0.2	0.9	1.8	3.0	4.1
Agricultural prices received by farmers	-0.2	-6.8	-13.5	5.2	17.4	12.3 [2]
Cost of construction	6.1	3.1	4.0	5.3	5.1	..
Labour	11.1	6.0	6.0	7.8	7.0	..
Materials	1.5	-0.8	1.5	2.7	3.1	..
Import prices of goods [3]	-2.9	-3.0	3.7	5.9	3.5	7.9
of which:						
Excluding energy	-2.8	-1.6	5.3	6.1	4.4	9.2
Memorandum item:						
GDP price deflator	7.0	6.5		4.5		

1. Break in series in December 1992.
2. January 1994.
3. The data are based on customs reports.
Source: Ministry of Economy and Finance, Síntesis Mensual de Indicadores Económicos and Bank of Spain, Boletín Estadístico.

positive development, considering that inflation stickiness in the service sectors and the associated wide inflation gap between goods and services had been particular characteristics of the strong inflation pressures and expectations in Spain since the mid-1980s.[8] In addition to a change in inflation expectations related to the generalised slack, the decline in inflation in non-tradeables was also affected by specific policy initiatives. In order to stem rapidly growing health costs, the authorities brought pressure to bear on producers and distributors of pharmaceutical products, so that health prices increased by only 4.6 per cent in the twelve months to end-1993, less than half the previous two years' increases.[9]

The rapid decline in the balance of payments deficit

After remaining at the high level of 3¹/₄ per cent of GDP for four consecutive years, the current balance of payments deficit fell to less than 1 per cent of GDP in 1993 (Table 5). Even allowing for some distortions in trade figures, the decline represents one of the fastest external adjustments in the OECD.[10] This significant improvement is due to the much sharper cyclical contraction of domestic demand in Spain than in its trading partners and the significant gains in external competitiveness following the 1992 and 1993 devaluations of the peseta, which boosted

Table 5. **The current balance of payments**

Pesetas billion

	1990	1991	1992	1993
Trade balance[1]	−2 964	−3 159	−3 089	−1 944
(per cent of GDP)	(−5.9)	(−5.8)	(−5.2)	(−3.2)
Exports	5 656	6 225	6 757	7 703
Imports	8 620	9 384	9 846	9 647
Non-factor services				
(excluding tourism)	−248	−265	−435	−463
Credits	950	1 056	1 185	1 440
Debits	1 199	1 321	1 620	1 903
Tourism	1 449	1 518	1 699	1 875
Net factor income[2]	−359	−445	−588	−572
Net transfers	440	628	609	594
Current balance	−1 683	−1 724	−1 803	−510
(per cent of GDP)	(−3.4)	(−3.1)	(−3.1)	(−0.8)
Memorandum items:				
US$ billion				
Trade balance	−32.07	−33.13	−35.45	−15.64
Current balance	−15.72	−16.02	−19.07	−5.59
	Per cent change			
Terms of trade, goods[3]	2.0	1.4	2.0	−0.3
Volume goods				
Exports	7.3	10.0	6.1	11.5
Imports	7.2	9.8	5.4	−4.2

1.   FOB.
2.   Investment and labour income.
3.   National accounts basis, which differ somewhat from customs basis.
Source: Bank of Spain, *Boletín Económico* and Ministry of Economy and Finance, *Síntesis Mensual de Indicadores Económicos.*

net export volumes (Diagram 2). Moreover, the deterioration in the terms of trade for goods was surprisingly small (less than 1 per cent) considering the devaluation of the peseta. This was made possible by weak commodity prices in world markets and price restraint of OECD exporters, and by the fact that depreciation was in part recuperated by increasing export prices, in order to compensate for squeezed profit margins in the domestic market.

Thanks to the exchange rate adjustments, relative unit labour costs declined by about 20 per cent between mid-1992 and end-1993, thereby falling back to the 1988 level (Diagram 3). Thus, despite the marked deceleration in export market growth, export volumes rose by some 10 per cent in 1993. Reflecting the contraction of domestic demand, notably of components with high import content, and improved competitiveness, there was a sizeable fall in import volumes of capital goods (24 per cent) and of non-food consumer goods (13 per cent), which largely explain the fall in total import volumes. Export/import coverage rose to 76 per cent in 1993 from 64 per cent on average in the previous five years, and for finished manufactured goods 91 per cent from 69 per cent. Apart from lower domestic demand pressures, this jump has also been made possible by the considerable investment in industry since the mid-1980s, as a result of which both overall industrial capacity has increased and product composition improved. Indeed, Spain's share in total OECD exports for medium and high technology products increased by two-thirds and four-fifths respectively since the mid-1980s.

There was also a significant rise in the services' surplus. In particular, there was a further large rise in tourism earnings, but also the number of Spanish tourists abroad fell by 11 per cent. In addition to the favourable effects of the depreciation of the peseta, there was a diversion of tourism towards Spain because of political problems in a few Mediterranean countries. The increment in the services' surplus more than offset the rise in net factor income payments abroad (reflecting the growth in net debt coupled with high interest rates), so that the invisible surplus also widened somewhat.

A new classification of the capital account items was introduced in 1993 and the 1990-92 figures were adjusted accordingly, but not the figures for earlier years, so that a comparison over a longer period is difficult. Comparing with 1990-92 there were large shifts in capital account components in 1993. The downward trend in foreign direct investment after 1990 (when it peaked at $14 billion) continued at a slower pace in 1993, as suggested by the decline in

21

Diagram 2. **THE EXCHANGE RATE**

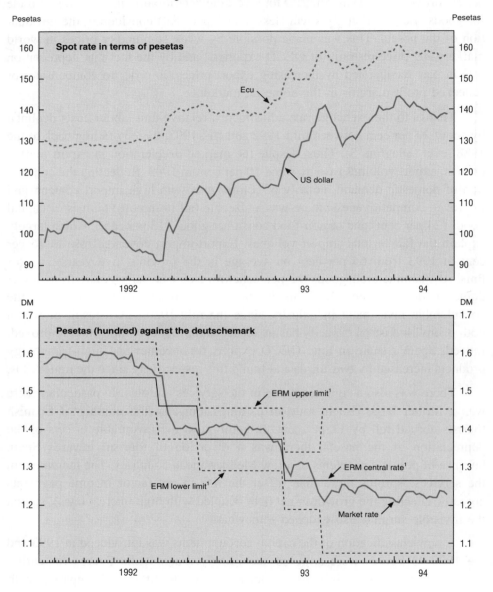

1. The exchange rate bands in the ERM were increased from 6 to 15 per cent in August 1993.
Source: OECD.

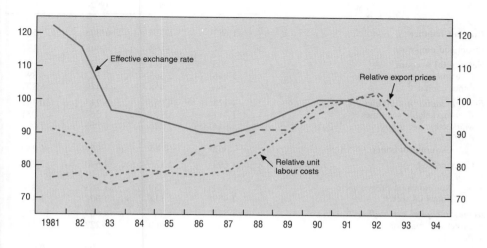

Diagram 3. **EXTERNAL COMPETITIVENESS**
1991 = 100

Source: OECD estimates.

foreign investment in non-marketable securities (Table 6). By contrast portfolio investment, as indicated by the movement in marketable securities, surged. In particular, reflecting favourable prospects for sizeable capital gains from the expected fall in interest rates, foreign investment into government paper, mainly bonds, rose to about Ptas 6 trillion (some $50 billion, ten times the average of the previous five years). However, foreigners wishing to avoid the exchange rate risk largely financed these purchases with short-term peseta loans provided by domestic financial institutions. This is seen in the equally steep growth of Spanish financial (short-term) loans to foreigners. Another new feature is the marked growth of Spanish investments abroad, notably in securities and it indicates the growing integration of Spain into the world economy. Official foreign exchange reserves, after peaking at $66 billion in 1991, declined steadily to $45 billion in the second quarter of 1993 and have broadly stabilised at that level since.

23

Table 6. The capital account: balance of payments

Cash basis, pesetas billion

	1990	1991	1992	1993
Current balance	−1 683	−1 724	−1 803	−510
Errors and omissions	87	−108	−608	−139
Net capital account [1]	2 306	3 321	633	83
Investment	1 946	2 863	2 122	6 890
Other capital	360	458	−1 489	−6 807
Foreign capital net inflows [2]	4 128	4 756	5 243	10 361
Non-marketable securities [3]	1 411	1 294	1 367	1 031
Marketable securities	1 024	2 276	1 256	7 089
of which:				
Government paper	353	1645	957	6 282
Other capital	1 693	1 186	2 620	2 241
of which:				
Non-financial private sector	234	459	1 263	810
Financial sector	1 459	818	1 357	1 431
Domestic capital net outflows [4]	1 822	1 435	4 609	10 278
Direct and real estate	351	460	222	312
Portfolio	138	247	278	918
Other capital	1 333	728	4 109	9 048
of which:				
Non-financial private sector, short-term capital	436	401	1 067	967
Financial sector, Repos	..	..	921	3 214
Financial sector, other short-term instruments	699	216	1 937	4 679
Change in official reserves (+ = decrease)	−710	−1 489	1778	566

1. Reserves are excluded.
2. Change in liabilities vis-à-vis the external sector.
3. Including real estate and other direct investment.
4. Change in assets vis-à-vis the external sector.
Source: Bank of Spain, *Boletín Económico.*

II. Economic policies

Macroeconomic policies

Deepening recession in Spain and in its main trading partners, the periodic attacks against the peseta during 1992 and 1993, and the need to pursue fiscal consolidation and disinflation made 1993 a very difficult year for policy makers. Moreover, 1993 was an electoral year, causing inevitable delays in the implementation of many macroeconomic measures and structural reforms. It is not surprising, therefore, that Spain, as a number of other OECD countries, missed many of its policy targets in 1993. Instead of the budgeted decline, the general government deficit leaped by 3 percentage points to a record 7¼ per cent of GDP in 1993. ALP (the wider monetary aggregate) overshot its target by 1 percentage point in 1993, despite slower nominal GDP growth than initially assumed. The peseta had to be devalued by 8 per cent in May 1993, following 6 per cent in November and 5 per cent in September 1992.

However, it would be wrong to conclude that the fiscal and monetary policy stance eased overall in 1993. On the fiscal side, the structural primary budget deficit was stable in 1993 according to Secretariat estimates, and it would have declined a little had it not been for deferred payments pertaining to earlier years and the delays in collecting VAT under the new reporting system. Indeed, important tax raising measures were introduced in 1992 and 1993 (e.g. the standard VAT rate passed from 12 to 15 per cent, the special taxes on hydrocarbons, tobacco and alcoholic beverages were significantly increased, and personal tax and social security contribution rates were also raised somewhat) and unemployment benefits were reduced. The net tax yield from these measures is equivalent to almost 2 per cent of GDP on a full year basis. The high rate of growth of ALP, the principal monetary target, also masks the depressive impact of monetary policy on private sector activity. Real interest rates were very high in

1993 as a whole and the growth of domestic credit to the private sector slowed markedly, well below the growth of nominal GDP.

The policy mix is better balanced in 1994. Fiscal policy has been tightened while monetary conditions eased. Moreover, the Government recently announced that additional measures will be introduced soon in order to put the budget deficit and debt back on a path consistent with the Maastricht Treaty's fiscal targets. Simultaneously with fiscal consolidation, the Government has placed great emphasis on structural policies, and presented a series of draft laws aimed at increasing labour market flexibility considerably (see Part IV) and deregulating other sectors.

Table 7. **General government accounts** [1]

National accounts definitions, pesetas billion

	1990	1991	1992[2]	1993[2]
Current revenue	19 002	21 171	23 617	24 203
Direct taxes	6 018	6 605	7 289	7 216
Households	4 298	4 964	5 746	5 832
Business	1 720	1 641	1 543	1 384
Indirect taxes	4 976	5 400	6 036	5 734
Social security contributions	6 537	7 256	8 236	8 771
Other	1 471	1 910	2 056	2 482
Current expenditure	18 475	21 268	23 851	26 095
Public consumption	7 756	8 808	9 901	10 467
of which:				
Wages and salaries	5 566	6 317	7 146	7 489
Social security benefits	7 221	8 367	9 530	10 578
Interest payments	1 776	2 173	2 490	2 938
Current transfers and other	1 723	1 920	1 930	2 112
Net saving	527	−96	−234	−1 892
Gross saving	1 035	478	386	−1 148
(per cent of GDP)	(2.1)	(0.9)	(0.7)	(−1.9)
Fixed investment	2 493	2 723	2 536	2 635
Net capital transfer payments	416	392	411	511
Net lending (+) or net borrowing (−)	−1 963	−2 699	−2 623	−4 374
(per cent of GDP)	(−3.9)	(−4.9)	(−4.5)	(−7.2)

1. Because of rounding, figures may not add up to total.
2. Provisional.
Source: Data submitted by national authorities, OECD, *National Accounts* and OECD estimates.

Fiscal policy

The 1993 Budget outcome

There were large deviations between projections and outcome in the central government and social security system's revenues and outlays for 1993 on a cash basis. Except for the doubling of property income compared with plans (in part due to the Bank of Spain's extraordinary profits generated by the devaluation), other revenue categories recorded sizeable shortfalls (in relation to the budget), considerably greater than in 1992, and two important taxes even had negative growth rates (Table 7). Particularly large was the shortfall in VAT receipts (16 per cent), largely explained by the marked fall in sales of consumer durables, which have relatively high VAT rates. In addition, one-off factors depressed net VAT receipts in 1993: VAT refunds due in 1992 were shifted to 1993; because of financial difficulties, many firms delayed the payment of VAT; under the new system the period for VAT payments on imports has been considerably extended; and the lifting of customs controls may also have increased fraud, so that imports and related taxes may be under-reported and exports over-reported. In total, VAT receipts in 1993 fell back to nearly the 1991 level. The shortfalls in corporate taxes and personal income tax receipts were also large (9 and 7 per cent respectively) because of the weakening of activity; in addition, the budget may not have properly assessed the impact of the earlier years' declines in profits, and tax evasion may have also increased.[11] The shortfall in social security contribution receipts was smaller (3 per cent), as the faster rise in average wages than budgeted partly offset the steeper fall in employment. Reflecting an increase of 0.5 per cent in unemployment contribution rates and an increase in the maximum wage ceiling upon which contributions are paid, social security contributions together with specific taxes (which were also subject to tax rate increases) were the only tax items to grow faster than nominal GDP. To sum up, state and social security receipts grew by a little over 3 per cent in 1993; however, excluding the Bank of Spain's extraordinary profits and privatisation receipts, they were broadly stable in 1993, with the tax/GDP ratio also falling from just over 31 per cent in 1992 to 30¼ per cent in 1993.

Slippage was also considerable on the spending side. Central government and social security spending together grew by 16 per cent in 1993, with all main components registering large overruns (Table 8). The planned wage freeze was

Table 8. **Central government and social security balances**

Pesetas billion

	1992		1993		1994
	Cash	National accounts	Cash	National accounts	Budget, cash
State	-1 867	-1 418	-3 774	-3 553	-3 297
(per cent of GDP)	(-3.2)	(-2.4)	(-6.2)	(-5.8)	(-5.2)
Other organisations		-9			
Social security system		-470		-176	-349
INEM		-52		430	
Other		-418		-606	
Total balance		-1 897		-3 699	-3 646
(per cent of GDP)[1]		(-3.2)		(-6.1)	(-5.7)
Memorandum item:					
State borrowing requirement					
(per cent of GDP)[2]	(4.4)	(4.4)	(7.6)	(7.9)	

1. The total balance on a national accounts basis was 3.1 per cent in 1990 and 3.3 per cent in 1991.
2. 4 per cent in 1990 and 3.9 per cent in 1991.
Source: National authorities.

not fully implemented and wages of certain categories were raised (in part because of the reclassification of administrative jobs), but on the other hand employment declined by 2 per cent in 1993. Non-wage consumption overshot its budget level by as much as 27 per cent, which made for an increase in State consumption by 6 per cent in 1993. The sharp rise in unemployment and other benefits also made for a rise in social welfare spending by 12 per cent, some 7 percentage points faster than budgeted. However, excluding payments to cover previous years' deficits of the unemployment account of the National Employment Agency (INEM) and of the National Health System (amounting to 1 per cent of GDP), growth in social welfare spending was around 10 per cent. It is worth mentioning that following the 1992 measures to shift the financing of temporary sick leave from the budget to firms, spending on this item declined by 4 per cent in 1993.[12] But this was partly offset by a continuing steep growth (by around 31 per cent in both 1992 and 1993) in temporary disability payments (mainly to those having exhausted their right to receive sick leave payments), suggesting growing abuse in this area too. Interest payments increased also somewhat faster than budgeted so that they continued to increase rapidly as a share of GDP, from 2.9 per cent in 1991 and 3.4 per cent in 1992 to 4.0 per cent in 1993.

State transfers also grew fast in 1993 to finance regional governments and local authorities as well as to cover the growing losses of state companies (Table 9). In addition to subsidies and capital transfers, the State regularly assumes debts of various public companies and organisations which cannot service them, and also increases its equity participation and/or gives loans, including to companies in financial difficulty. The corresponding sums are not immediately shown in the income and outlay accounts but are included in the borrowing requirement, which has exceeded the deficit by as much as 1 1/4 per cent of GDP on average in the last couple of years, and are then added to the existing debt thereby augmenting future debt servicing and deficits.

In 1992 an agreement was reached between the Government and Regions to reduce the latters' deficit from 1 1/2 per cent of GDP in 1991 and 1 1/4 per cent in 1992 to less than 1 per cent in 1993 and to 1/4 per cent of GDP in 1996.[13] However, it seems that in 1993 regional governments (and municipalities) gave relatively high wage rises and hired more people, while revenues from *ceded* taxes (taxes raised directly by the regions, mainly on real estate transactions and donations) fell somewhat reflecting the weakness in the real estate market. In addition, as revenues through the *participation in state receipts* (the other main component of tax revenues) were broadly stagnant, Regions' total tax and property income revenues seem to have declined in 1993. This was partly offset by a marked rise in State transfers to Regions (their level was 15 per cent more than budgeted), partly to finance new activities (*i.e.* after budgets were voted), the transferred items from the central government and part of their unanticipated deficit. In total, the deficit of Regions, as suggested by the continuing strong growth of over 20 per cent in indebtedness, does not seem to have shrunk as a per cent of GDP or, at best very little, and this was, moreover, at the expense of a higher State deficit. Incomplete data on local authorities indicate that they also followed expansionary policies, and a few of them had difficulties in servicing their debt in 1993. The combined deficit of the Regions and local authorities in 1993, therefore, continued to exceed 1 per cent of GDP.

In total, the general government deficit on a national accounts basis reached 7 1/4 per cent of GDP in 1993, of which two-thirds is estimated to be structural (Diagram 4).[14] The 1993 increase in the overall deficit was the largest for many

Table 9. **The State budget**[1]

Cash basis, pesetas billion

	1990	1991	1992	1993 Budget	1993 Outcome[2]	1994 Budget
Total revenues	10 208	11 232	12 278	13 320	12 684	13 217
Direct taxes	4 992	5 538	5 986	6 442	5 978	6 048
of which:						
Households	3 464	4 093	4 631	5 105	4 743	5 122
Indirect taxes	4 021	4 242	4 845	5 156	4 511	4 957
of which:						
VAT	2 489	2 680	3 113	3 419	2 764	3 112
On oil	793	964	1 110	1 140	1 118	1 184
Transfers	564	471	420	767	542	909
Other revenues	631	981	1 027	955	1 653	1 303
Total expenditure	11 377	12 600	14 145	14 753	16 458	16 514
Consumption	2 478	2 737	2 822	2 834	2 992	3 001
Wages and salaries	2 164	2 373	2 464	2 510	2 582	2 647
Goods and services	314	364	358	324	410	354
Current transfers	5 607	6 154	7 526	7 802	9 059	8 791
Interest payments	1 428	1 593	2 001	2 342	2 409	2 862
Fixed investment	896	1 028	879	917	985	1 026
Capital transfers	968	1 088	917	858	1 013	835
Net overall balance	−1 170	−1 368	−1 867	−1 433	−3 774	−3 297
Borrowing requirement[3]	−1 986	−2 144	−2 608		−4 638	
Short-term debt[4]	1 116	−749	181		202	
Medium and long-term debt	587	2 038	1 119		6 298	
Bank of Spain[5]	−130	9	−114		−2 237	
Other	413	847	1 423		376	
Financed by foreign investors	385	1 770	178		2 858	

1. On an administrative basis. The State budget is by far the largest part of the central government budget, as it includes the subsidies to the social security system, which is part of the central government.
2. Official estimate.
3. Net change in financial liabilities. A negative figure indicates a deficit.
4. Short-term debt includes Treasury bills and Treasury notes.
5. Excluding Bank of Spain net purchases of government paper.
Source: Ministry of Economy and Finance, *Presentación de los Presupuestos Generales del Estado 1994*, Bank of Spain, *Boletín Estadístico* and *Cuentas Financieras de la Economía Española (1983-1992)* and OECD estimates.

years, and is mainly due to the recession, as underlined by the rise in the cyclical deficit of 2 per cent. The fast growth in interest payments, over which the government has very little control in the short term, accounted for the remaining part ($^3/_4$ per cent of GDP) of the rise in the deficit. Even so, the failure of the primary structural deficit to decline, despite discretionary tax rate increases and

Diagram 4. **GENERAL GOVERNMENT FINANCIAL BALANCES
AND FISCAL INDICATORS**[1]

Per cent of GDP

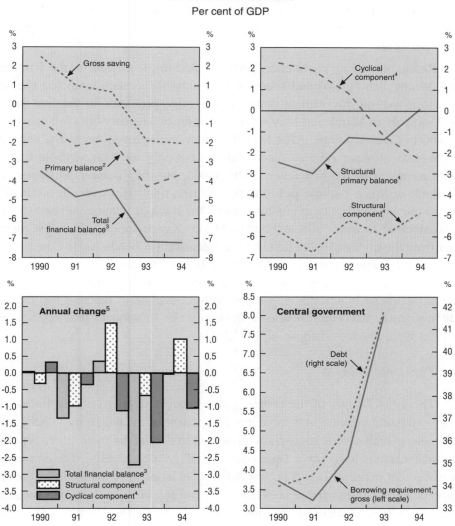

1. Figures for 1990 and 1991 have been adjusted for tax deferment; 1993 and 1994 are based on OECD projections.
2. Net lending plus net interest payments.
3. Net lending, national accounts basis.
4. As a per cent of potential GDP.
5. A positive sign indicates higher surpluses or lower deficits.
Source: OECD, *National accounts*, Ministry of Economy and Finance, and OECD estimates.

spending cuts, is disappointing and suggests growing tax evasion and abuse of the social security system. The State debt rose from 36¾ per cent of GDP in 1992 to 46 per cent in 1993, and the general government debt from 48½ per cent to 56 per cent.

Reflecting falling confidence, partly related to the turmoil in the Exchange Rate Mechanism (ERM) and speculation against the peseta, financing the high and rising central government deficit posed some problems in the first part of 1993, notably in March and May when new sales of Treasury bills fell considerably short of amortisations. After May the situation improved markedly, and sales of government paper were so successful that not only were the sizeable Bank of Spain advances of the first few months repaid, but the Treasury's balance with the Bank of Spain became positive, for the first time. However, in order to be able to operate efficiently in money markets the Bank of Spain continued to build up its stock of Treasury bills and bonds. Markets' expectations of a fall in interest rates from the high end-1992 level boosted demand for bonds, so that the stock of medium and longer-term debt in December 1993 was some 74 per cent above the end-1992 level, with foreign purchases accounting for two thirds of this increase. The attraction of bonds was accompanied by a decline in demand for Treasury bills during the first eight months, and, despite the subsequent pick up, net sales in 1993 were about half those of 1992.[15]

The 1994 Budget

The 1994 Budget of the central government is restrictive. Despite an officially estimated increase in the cyclical component of the deficit by ¾ per cent of GDP, the overall deficit is officially projected to decline by over ½ per cent on a national accounts basis (over 1 per cent of GDP on a cash basis). The consequent improvement in the structural budget deficit is planned to be achieved by containing expenditure. The narrow tax/GDP ratio and the broader definition including social security contributions are forecast to fall slightly to 17¼ per cent of GDP and 30 per cent of GDP. In addition to the non-indexation of personal income tax allowances and thresholds, unemployment benefits will be taxed for the first time, so that a small increase in the personal income tax/GDP ratio is expected. However, this is planned to be more than offset by lower corporate taxes, reflecting the downward trend in profits in earlier years and new higher amortisation allowances and fiscal incentives for training and investments. A sizeable increase is projected for indirect taxes, in particular VAT receipts (13 per cent). In addition to the pick up in sales of durable goods and cars, the 1994 rise is explained by the unwinding of the special factors which depressed VAT receipts in 1993.

Expenditure of the central government and the social security system (cash basis) is budgeted to remain roughly flat, and in relation to GDP to decline to 41½ per cent from 43½ per cent in 1992, and excluding interest payments to 37 per cent from 39½ per cent.[16] Excluding interest payments, which are again budgeted to rise fast, expenditure is budgeted to fall by more than 5 per cent in real terms. A large part of this decline is explained by the extraordinary spending in 1993, which will not be repeated in 1994. Moreover, the following measures were decided:

i) wages of public servants are frozen;

ii) only one government employee out of two who leave the public service will be replaced;

iii) non-wage consumption, which had risen markedly in 1993, will be drastically cut (by nearly 12 per cent in real terms). These cuts will affect especially the internal security, defence and education departments;

iv) capital transfers as well as current transfers to Regions and state owned companies will be cut, reflecting lower net losses in these sectors as a result of improved financial discipline and higher sales, as activity picks up;

v) structural measures taken in 1992-93 to abolish certain employment promotion and training schemes and to limit health expenditure are expected to produce sizeable savings in 1994, making for practically no change in the level of subsidies given for the first group of activities and only a small increase in spending on health; and

vi) to curb the steep trend-rise in pensions (from 9 per cent of GDP in 1990 to 10.5 per cent in 1993), the average pension will, as from 1994, be indexed to the projected inflation and not to the past 12-month inflation.

Moreover, in the face of the severe crisis in construction, companies in bidding for projects have been offering big discounts making for sizeable budgetary savings on this item. Furthermore, an increasing part of infrastructure investment will be financed by EC structural funds, thus further relieving the State's budget finances.

Regional budgets are also stated to be less expansionary in 1994. After rising by 17 per cent in 1992 and 10 per cent in 1993, total regional spending is budgeted to grow by some 5½ per cent in 1994, which, allowing for the continuing transfer of responsibilities, means that growth is closer to 5 per cent, only slightly faster than that projected for nominal GDP. In line with the central government's guidelines, wage growth should be small, but investment should continue to expand rapidly, partly financed by EC and State transfers. At the insistence of the more affluent Regions wishing to dispose freely of a larger proportion of the taxes they raise, the Regions' financing system has also been modified. As from 1994, 15 per cent of the personal income taxes raised in each Region will be transferred to the regional government. However, certain criteria have been established so that, at least at the beginning, the combined extra revenues accruing to all Regions will be limited.[17] It seems that the new system will also make for a speedier transfer of taxes from the State budget to the Regions.

The 1994 Budget again seems to be optimistic. As in the past, slippage in the implementation of policies announced may occur in 1994. The Government is studying new mechanisms in order to improve tax collection and expenditure controls, but, as these are planned to be introduced at a later stage, the 1994 Budget will not benefit.[18] The Secretariat projections show the general government deficit (on a national accounts basis) as a broadly stable proportion of GDP, but the structural deficit is projected to decline by 1 per cent.

Tight monetary conditions

Exchange rate stability and maintaining the peseta in the ERM have ranked high in monetary policy goals in the last few years, even though the peseta was devalued three times between September 1992 and May 1993 as a result of strong speculative attacks during the turmoil in the ERM. These goals have placed a heavy burden on monetary policy, in particular in the context of the rapidly rising budget deficit. In order to counter domestic and external destabilising forces, the authorities in mid-1992 reversed the downward trend in interest rates and maintained them at a very high level up to almost mid-1993. Combined with the fall in

Diagram 5. **INTEREST RATES**

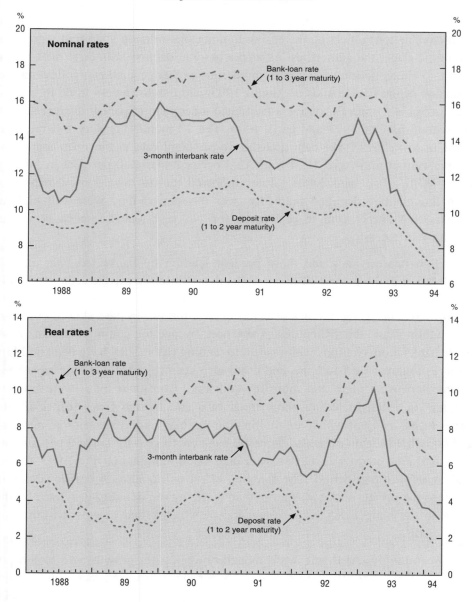

1. Nominal rates deflated by the consumer price index.
Source: OECD, *Main Economic Indicators* and *Financial Statistics.*

35

inflation, this pushed real interest rates up to the record level of 12 per cent (for loans with 1-3 year maturity) in early 1993 (Diagram 5). In May 1993 (after the third devaluation) reflecting the easing in domestic inflation and rapidly growing economic slack, the authorities initiated a gradual decline in interest rates.[19] The return to more normal conditions in foreign exchange markets, following the widening of the ERM bands in August 1993, and the downward trend in interest rates in Spain's main EC partners facilitated a decline in Spanish interest rates in the second half of 1993 and early 1994. The 12-month Treasury bill rate was brought down to 7.7 per cent and the 5-year bond rate in the open market to 8.3 per cent at mid-April 1994 from 12.3 per cent and 13.0 per cent in January 1993. With a lag, bank lending rates followed the downward movement. But even though they declined markedly over this period they were still high in March 1994 (7 per cent in real terms for 1-3 year loans), especially for an economy in recession.

High interest rates and more prudent lending by banks led to a marked deceleration in the growth of domestic bank credit to the private sector to barely 1¾ per cent in the 12 months to end-1993 from 6¾ per cent during 1992 (Table 10). The rising number of bankruptcies, the fall in the value of commercial buildings and the difficulties experienced by one big commercial bank have made banks more cautious with respect to lending risks. They have been building reserves to cover for bad loans and it has also been reported that they have been asking borrowers more and more for collateral. Consumer loans were broadly stagnant in 1993. Including commercial bills and foreign loans (especially of larger firms, many of which are multinational), total credit expansion to business and households again exceeded domestic bank credit growth, but at 2 per cent the growth of total credit was much slower than that of nominal GDP in 1993, for the first time for a long period. The damping effect on liquidity of the slowdown in credit to the private sector was more than offset by the liquidity generated by the surge in the budget deficit, the financing of which relied heavily on domestic bank credit.

Accordingly, ALP (the wide monetary aggregate) growth rose to 8.6 per cent in 1993 (above the target of 4.5-7.5 per cent), from 5.2 per cent in 1992 (Diagram 6). Considering that nominal GDP growth was slower than had been assumed when the targets were announced, the overshooting can be considered even greater than the above data indicate. In addition to the excessive liquidity

Table 10. **Monetary aggregates**

	1993 Ptas billion	1990	1991	1992	1993
		Per cent change, annual rate			
ALP[1]					
Target		6.5-9.5	7-11	8-11	4.5-7.5
Outturn	62 576	12.6	10.8	5.2	8.6
Net domestic credit to residents[2]	69 569	11.0	9.1	7.3	3.7
General government	19 939	13.0	3.6	9.0	9.9
Companies and households[3]	49 630	10.3	11.2	6.7	1.8
M1	16 168	19.4	12.3	−1.7	3.4
Currency	6 514	18.2	23.7	7.4	8.1
Sight deposits	9 654	20.0	6.9	−6.7	0.5
M3	58 578	13.2	10.8	4.7	9.1
Savings deposits	10 786	14.5	11.5	1.6	7.2
Time deposits	20 618	10.5	15.2	11.6	15.6
Other components of M3	11 006	7.7	1.4	6.8	8.1
of which:					
Repurchase agreements on public debt	8 659	9.3	−3.4	2.1	10.0
Other liquid assets	6 765	−0.1	17.4	10.4	19.2
Outright portfolio of short-term public debt[4]	5 096	7.2	33.8	16.6	20.6
Private-created liquid assets	1 669	−10.1	−9.2	−4.3	15.2
ALP[5]	65 343	11.9	11.4	5.2	10.1
Memorandum items:					
ALP2[6]	64 746	16.4	10.8	5.0	7.6
General government					
A. Domestic credit plus special and long-term debt held by residents	23 395	12.0	5.6	14.0	11.3
B. A plus foreign direct financing	29 082	13.3	14.6	13.3	20.9
Companies and households					
A. Domestic credit plus commercial paper	51 751	14.7	11.2	6.4	0.5
B. A plus foreign direct financing	56 035	14.6	12.3	8.7	2.1

1. Monthly average of daily data. ALP stands for liquid assets in the hands of the public, which includes M3, outright portfolio of short-term public debt, private asset transfer certificates, insurance transactions issued by savings banks, endorsed bills and guarantees on commercial paper.
2. Bank and money market transactions only.
3. Bi-monthly average of end-month data.
4. Including regional government treasury bills.
5. ALP components are based on end-month data.
6. ALP plus commercial paper, monthly average of daily data.
Source: Bank of Spain, *Boletín Estadístico.*

generated by the budget deficit, it seems that shifts in the composition of debt instruments also bloated ALP growth in 1993. A large part of the additional liquidity created is held by households (underlined by the rise in the household

Diagram 6. CREDIT AND MONETARY EXPANSION

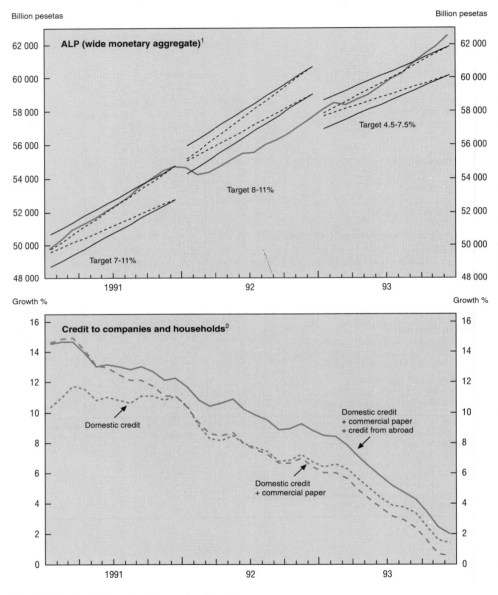

1. Monthly average of daily data, seasonally adjusted.
2. Average growth over 12 months.
Source: Bank of Spain, *Boletín Económico* and *Boletín Estadístico.*

38

saving rate and the fall in real investment), and households usually place a greater part of their financial assets with banks, in particular with saving banks, in the form of term deposits. Indeed, reflecting the wish of asset holders to benefit from the relatively high interest rates, overall term deposits increased by about 16 per cent in 1993, contributing nearly 50 per cent to the growth of ALP in 1993.

For 1994, a wide ALP target range of 3 to 7 per cent was fixed, due to several large uncertainties: first, the speed of decline in interest rates, influenced both by inflation trends in Spain and interest rates changes in the principal European Monetary System (EMS) countries; second, the possibility of further shifts between various debt instruments; and third, the assumptions of inflation and real growth underlying the monetary projections. This target is consistent with a projected domestic credit growth of 5 per cent for the private sector and 9.5 per cent for the government, provided also that the general government deficit falls to 6.4 per cent of GDP. Moreover, in assessing monetary conditions, the Bank of Spain will, as in the last few years, continue to supplement the information provided by the ALP with that provided by narrower monetary variables and will also monitor the yield curve, which, at this phase, captures market sentiment regarding future inflation. The rapid fall in interest rates until early 1994 considerably reduced the wide interest rate differential between Spain and its principal EMS partners (notably those with Germany from 5½ per cent for long-term government bonds at the end of 1992 to roughly 2 per cent in April 1994). This narrowing has practically exhausted the margin for further significant unilateral interest rate decreases in Spain, unless inflation falls further.[20] Rapid introduction of structural reforms and budget deficit reduction, would also help to lower interest rates further. The independence to be given to the Bank of Spain by mid-1994 should reinforce the credibility of the anti-inflationary policy, but this is not expected to affect the actual conduct of monetary policy significantly in 1994.

Structural policies

Competition policy

The Franquist regime's corporatist philosophy and the central role of the administration in numerous aspects of economic life have left their marks in

Spain, most visibly in the labour market (see Part IV), but also in the area of competition and direct state intervention in the productive process. The resulting inefficiencies have been an important factor behind high inflation in the last fifteen years and have led to considerable waste of resources.[21] A significant turn was made in 1989, when a new competition law was voted, strengthening the independence of the *Competition Court* and, at the same time, increasing the responsibilities of the (government) *Service for the Defence of Competition.* The Court, in the last few years, has prepared comprehensive reports attacking the lack of competition in many areas and suggested appropriate changes which, however, cannot be made without new laws, and has initiated procedures against firms breaking competition rules and has imposed fines. The educational role of the Court is also very important. By bringing to the attention of the public the absence of competitive conditions in key areas and the deleterious effects of weak competition on economic performance, the Court has opened the debate on issues which were largely ignored before.

The number of cases treated and terminated by the Competition Court increased considerably in 1993 (by one-half compared with 1992).[22] Furthermore, studies and investigations for anti-competitive practices on a number of activities (*e.g.* the vegetable oil market, dairy sector, elevator installation and maintenance, pharmacies, publishing, book prices, gasoline prices, and road oil transport) were initiated in 1993. At the request of the Ministry of Finance, the Court has also given its judgement on mergers, and in all cases the Government has implemented the Court's proposals.

Concerning anti-competitive practices and rigidities in general, liberal professions are notorious. Regarding professional organisations; membership is obligatory in order to practice, there are barriers to entry, competition within a set geographical area (*e.g.* a municipality or province) is severely restricted and minimum price fixing is common.[23] Following the Court's "Report on Free Professional Practice", published in 1992, a draft law was prepared in the spring of 1993 eliminating flagrant anti-competitive rules. Unfortunately, because of imminent elections, legislative procedure was interrupted and after the elections the draft-law was not resubmitted to Parliament. Although policies in general are moving in the direction of deregulation, the Government presented a draft law opening the door for regional authorities to considerably restrict existing flexibility in shopping hours. This change, which runs counter to the general trend in the

OECD area, will weaken competitive forces, and therefore make disinflation even more difficult.

Greater emphasis is now put on derestriction and privatisation of state monopolies in order to inject greater competition and promote efficiency. Since 1993, the monopoly of Iberia on domestic flights has been broken (so that, for example, the arrival in 1994 of a new operator in the shuttle service Madrid-Barcelona led to a significant price reduction); maritime transport has been partly liberalised; and specific road transport services have been deregulated. Moreover, value-added telecommunications services were partly liberalised, but the tele-communications monopoly of Telefonica for domestic and international connec-tions was, with the agreement of the EC, extended to 2002. The Court considers that, in line with the EC directives, an early liberalisation in cable TV transmis-sion, mobile phones, data transmission networks and communication between satellites and ground stations for channelling long distance calls, will be very beneficial for users and will also exert pressure on Telefonica to prepare itself better for intense competition after 2002. Likewise, big efficiency gains can be reaped by stimulating competition in the generation of electricity, oil distribution and the provision of services provided by municipalities.

Other structural issues

Restructuring of state companies (including closure of some plants in min-ing, iron and steel, and shipbuilding) continued in 1993. Despite this, the losses of *Instituto Nacional de Industria* (INI, the state holding company) and other state companies (*e.g.* railways) are likely to be much higher than earlier, probably reaching almost 1 per cent of GDP. Iberia losses were almost double the 1992 level. Continuous bailing-out of state, regional and municipal companies is not conducive to increasing financial discipline, which also explains that, despite their losses and the Government's directives for wage moderation, wage increases in many of these companies continued to be fairly high in the last few years. Contrary to the performance of the INI group, the profits of Argentaria (the state held company comprising a number of banks, including the Post Office Savings Bank) may have increased by as much as 15 per cent in 1993. The good record of Argentaria also explains the oversubscription by foreign and domestic investors of the shares issued, so that privatisation proceeds from this source alone amounted to 0.1 per cent of GDP. Partial privatisation of Repsol, the state

41

company in oil distribution, also provided an additional 0.1 per cent of GDP in 1993 and 0.3 per cent in 1992.

In January 1994 the Government also presented a bill modifying residential and commercial rent and lease arrangements. The intention of the legislator is to gradually liberalise the market for old leases (dating from before 1985), bringing regulated rents, which are now sometimes 90 per cent below those of new leases, slowly back to market-related levels over the next ten years. Moreover, the proposed legislation considerably curbs the possibility of transferring leases to descendants. On the other hand, the bill proposes a minimum of four years for new leases, whereas under existing arrangements the contracting parties were free to set the duration of the lease. Even though owners sometimes abuse their power by not prolonging a short-term lease, the existing more flexible arrangements for new leases facilitate labour mobility, which is not the case with obligatory long-term leases.

III.   Economic outlook for 1994-1995

Recent data suggest that the economy was still weak overall in the beginning of 1994, but activity was picking up. Industrial production, which reached the trough in mid-1993, has been on a slow upward trend since then, and sales of durables, which had declined rapidly through 1993, also started to grow in the first quarter of 1994, while the steep rise in registered unemployment came to a halt in February-April 1994. Business surveys also showed less pessimism than in 1992 and 1993, in particular future prospects swung from a negative figure until the end of 1993 to a positive one in early 1994 (Diagram 7). Another positive element is a marked decline in the number of enterprises considering that stock levels are high, which suggests that stock changes will not again be a drag on GDP in 1994. As for households, the depressed confidence level was broadly stationary in the last eighteen months to the first quarter of 1994, but concern about unemployment seems to be receding.

The more balanced policy mix in 1994 is expected to strengthen the forces of recovery in the course of the year. The marked decline in interest rates since the spring of 1993 is expected to provide a big relief to firms' cashflow. However, at this stage, this is unlikely to be immediately translated into a marked increase in demand, as it would mainly be used to strengthen firms' balance sheets. Even though the budget targets may not be achieved in full and the deficit is not likely to decline, an improvement (1 per cent of GDP) in the primary structural deficit is projected. Furthermore, the fall in the total deficit on a cash basis, which is the measure most relevant for financial markets, may reach 1 per cent of GDP. The fiscal tightening, on the one hand, would have a direct restrictive effect on activity and damp inflation pressures, but, on the other, would boost confidence and make room for a fall in interest rates. Likewise, the proposed labour market reforms are also expected to boost business confidence, but their positive effects will be perceived gradually.

Diagram 7. **BUSINESS SURVEYS (INDUSTRY)**

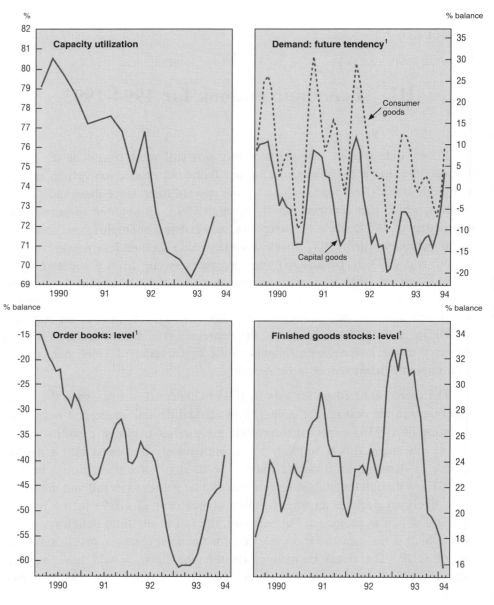

1. Per cent, balance of replies.
Source: Ministry of Industry, Trade and Tourism, and OECD, *Main Economic Indicators.*

Table 11. **Underlying assumptions for 1994 and 1995**

Per cent change, annual rate

	1992	1993	1994	1995
	External sector			
Market growth of manufactures	4.9	−2.2	4.6	6.6
Effective exchange rate of the peseta	−2.3	−12.1	−7.7	0.2
Import price of goods (customs basis)	−3.0	5.9	3.3	2.1
OECD import price of crude oil (US$ per barrel)	(17.5)	(15.4)	(13.3)	(13.5)
	Domestic sector			
Business sector, compensation per employee	8.9	7.4	4.6	3.5
Labour force growth	0.5	1.1	1.2	0.9
General government real fixed investment	−9.2	0.4	2.7	2.6
Short-term interest rates	(13.3)	(11.7)	(8.5)	(7.4)

Source: OECD estimates.

The external environment is also more favourable than it was in early 1993. Exchange rate turbulence has subsided. Spanish export markets are projected to grow faster in 1994, so that exports should again be an important element of support to growth (Table 11). Continuing disinflation in Spain's trading partners will continue to exert downward pressure on Spanish inflation, and, together with the favourable impact from low oil prices, could more than offset the increase in all other commodity prices.

Reflecting the Government's resolve to contain public spending, wage growth in the general government is expected to decelerate to around 3 per cent. Despite the marked increase in unemployment, the deceleration in wages in the business sector is likely to be smaller, reflecting the weight given to the most recent inflation trends in wage negotiations. Accordingly, wage settlements may be about 3½-4 per cent in 1994 as a whole, as suggested by recent agreements (Table 12).[24] Including the carry over from 1993 and higher social security contributions, the compensation per employee in the business sector is assumed to grow overall by just over 4½ per cent in 1994, 2¾ percentage points slower than in 1993. After the surge in 1993, labour productivity growth is expected to moderate to 2½ per cent, giving an increase in unit labour costs in the non-farm

Table 12. **Recent indicators**

	1992	1993	1993 Nov.	1993 Dec.	1994 Jan.	1994 Feb.	March
	(1992 = 100, seasonally adjusted)						
Manufacturing production	100.0	95.5	96.6	101.9	95.8	100.5	..
Registered unemployed	100.0	112.4	117.0	117.7	119.5	119.1	119.0
Retail sales, volume	100.0	91.4	88.0	88.8	91.0	88.3	96.7
of which: non food	100.0	88.5	84.2	85.1	89.5	85.8	96.1
Car registrations	100.0	77.0	77.4	85.9	69.2	81.2	94.6
	Percentage change over previous year						
Consumer prices[1]	5.9	4.6	4.7	4.9	5.0	5.0	5.0
of which: non food	7.1	6.2	5.3	5.2	5.2	5.0	4.8
Wage settlements	7.2	6.1	5.6	..	..	4.2	..
ALP[1]	6.3	7.7	8.4	8.6	8.1	6.7	7.1
Bank credit to the private sector	7.9	4.2	1.8	1.8	1.7	1.2	1.7
Exports of goods[2]	6.1	14.7	17.9	32.4	50.8	47.7	36.2
of which: volume	5.5	9.6	13.4	28.3	45.7	41.8	30.2
Imports of goods[2]	5.5	-2.0	10.1	19.3	24.4	37.0	23.7
of which: volume	8.8	-7.5	3.3	15.3	18.6	28.4	14.6
	Pesetas billion						
Trade deficit[2]	-3 599.3	-2 422.3	-226.7	-314.4	-79.0	-186.9	-100.4

1. In April 1994 the percentage change over twelve months for consumer prices and ALP was 4.9 and 6.9 per cent respectively.
2. Customs basis, seasonally adjusted data. Because of a new reporting system the series are somewhat distorted, in particular, per cent changes in the first months of 1994 overstate the actual trends.
Source: Ministry of Economy and Finance, *Síntesis Mensual de Indicadores Económicos.*

business sector of 2 per cent in 1994. On the assumption that profit margins will increase somewhat and that budgeted increases in indirect taxes are realised, the GDP price deflator is projected to rise by 3³/₄ per cent in 1994. However, including the depreciation-induced strong rises in import prices, consumer price inflation is expected to be almost 4¹/₂ per cent in 1994 as a whole, but falling to 3³/₄ per cent towards the end of the year.[25]

Except for social transfers, which in line with budget plans are again projected to rise faster than prices, all other household income components are projected to increase more slowly than consumer prices (because of the fall in employment, in real wages and in interest rates), so that gross household income should decline in real terms. This, coupled with a faster increase in personal taxes, would make for a small decline in real household disposable income. However, it is assumed that, as confidence improves, the saving rate will decline from the exceptionally high 1993 level, so that private consumption may increase a little (Table 13). Government consumption is expected to decline, for the first time in the last forty years, as the budget restrictions on hiring and outlays on goods and services are put into effect. Government investment is likely to rise, as many of the numerous and large infrastructure projects tendered for in 1993 start

Table 13. **Short-term prospects**

OECD projections

	1993	1994	1995
	Per cent change, annual rate		
Private consumption	-2.3	0.7	2.7
Government consumption	1.6	-0.2	0.5
Gross fixed investment	-10.3	-2.1	5.0
Total domestic demand	-3.6	0.0	2.9
Exports of goods and services	8.8	9.9	8.9
Imports of goods and services	-3.2	4.5	9.1
Foreign balance [1]	2.9	1.1	-0.3
GDP at constant prices	-1.0	1.2	2.7
GDP price deflator	4.5	3.8	3.3
Private consumption deflator	5.1	4.5	3.4
Memorandum items:			
Non-farm business sector			
Unit labour costs	3.8	2.0	2.0
Productivity	3.5	2.5	1.5
Employment	-4.3	-1.2	0.7
Unemployment rate (per cent)	(22.7)	(24.5)	(24.4)
	Per cent of GDP		
Current external balance [2]	-0.8	-0.5	-0.8
Government net lending [3]	-7.2	-7.1	-5.9
of which:			
Gross saving	-1.9	-1.9	-0.8
Primary balance	-2.4	-1.9	-0.7

1. Contribution to growth of GDP.
2. On a transactions basis.
3. A minus sign indicates a deficit.
Source: OECD estimates.

Diagram 8. CONJUNCTURAL INDICATORS
Seasonally adjusted

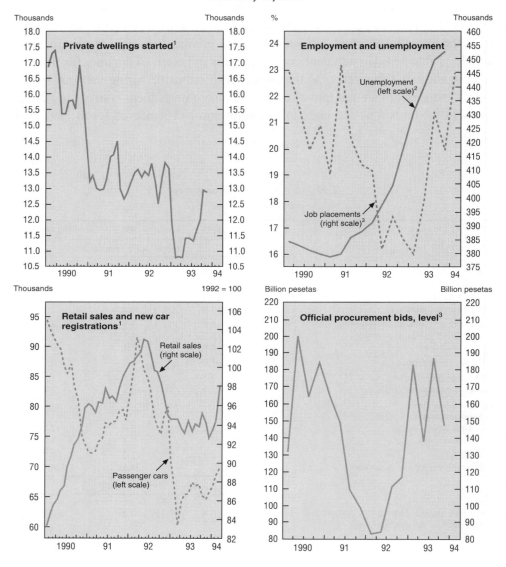

1. Three-month moving average centred on last month.
2. Registered unemployment as a per cent of total labour force.
3. Quarterly average of monthly data.
Source: Ministry of Economy and Finance, and other national sources.

to be constructed, becoming a strong element of support to the recovery (Diagram 8).

In line with the downward trend in housing starts in 1993, residential investment is projected to fall in 1994, but much slower than in 1992 and 1993. The large margins of unutilized capacity at the end of 1993 and still low profit rates suggest that business investment is likely to decline somewhat further in 1994. Total domestic demand may broadly stabilise. But, underpinned by the lagged effects of the marked improvement in competitiveness in 1992 and 1993, a further strong growth in net exports is projected. GDP should, therefore, rise by just over 1 per cent in 1994 as a whole, and by nearly 2 per cent during the year. As suggested by recent trends, manufacturing output, boosted by net exports, is also projected to grow in 1994, following three years of decline.

As seen in Diagram 9, the Spanish economy, under normal conditions, creates employment only when the rate of growth of GDP is at least around $2\frac{1}{2}$ per cent, and this rate is unlikely to be reached in 1994, so that employment is likely to fall again in 1994. Indeed, as redundancy notifications by some large-sized companies indicate, labour hoarding has not been completely eliminated following the sizeable labour shake-out in 1992 and 1993, when cumulatively some 900 000 jobs were destroyed. On the other hand, recruitment under the new apprenticeship contracts has risen markedly in the first quarter of 1994 (55 000), so that even if young apprentices to some extent replace older workers, this scheme overall seems to have a strong net employment creation effect (see Part IV). This, together with the positive effects of the labour market reforms (planned to be introduced in mid-1994), is expected to limit the decline in employment to some 1 per cent in 1994. Even so, the rate of unemployment is projected to reach $24\frac{1}{2}$ per cent in 1994 as a whole and close to 25 per cent at the end of the year.

Continuing slack, improved competitiveness and a recovery in activity in the OECD area would make for further strong growth in export volumes. Reflecting the pick up in private consumption and the weakening effects from the 1992-93 depreciation of the peseta, import volumes are expected to rise in 1994, as foreshadowed by the trend of the last few months of 1993. In total, the trade deficit in real terms is likely to narrow and more than offset the deterioration in the terms of trade, so that a further decline in the trade deficit (in value) is projected. Tourism earnings are again expected to rise, which, together with the

Diagram 9. **NON-FARM GDP GROWTH AND EMPLOYMENT CREATION (1980-93)**

Percentage change over same quarter of previous year

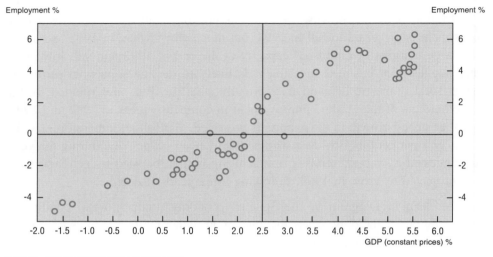

Source: Ministry of Economy and Finance.

higher EC transfers, would largely offset the increase in net factor payments abroad, so that the invisible balance may rise a little. On this basis the current balance of payments deficit is projected to decline in 1994.

The improvement in economic fundamentals (notably a lower inflation, rising profit rates and a sound balance of payments) and a small fall in real interest rates coupled with financial balances restructuring in 1994 will create promising conditions for accelerated growth in 1995. Likewise, GDP growth is projected to gather pace in OECD Europe and Japan. This is likely to affect primarily business investment, which, after falling by 17 per cent in the three years to 1994, is projected to show a strong recovery in 1995. Private consumption should also rise fast, supported by lower real interest rates and the marked fall in households' net financial liabilities in the preceding three years. GDP may thus grow by about 2³/₄ per cent in 1995 as a whole and 3³/₄ per cent during 1995, accompanied by net employment creation after three years of substantial job losses. Unemployment will, however, remain high and lead to further wage de-escalation, so that consumer price inflation could fall to less than 3 per cent towards the end of 1995. The current balance of payments deficit is expected to increase somewhat in 1995, but it should remain relatively small and be more than covered by inflows of foreign direct investment.

In 1995, after three years of growing slack, the growth of GDP is projected nearly to reach its potential and inflation to have been brought under control. However, there is a risk that unions' resistance to labour market reforms may disturb the favourable climate for wage moderation, with private wage settlements in 1994 higher than projected. Furthermore, it cannot be excluded that the recent export/import price moderation masks to some extent suppressed inflation, which will be liberated when the recovery gathers pace. Accordingly, there are upside risks for inflation and downside risks for GDP growth, notably that a wage-induced erosion of the recent substantial gains in competitiveness will push the unemployment rate even higher than the 25 per cent. Furthermore, the projections for moderate non-inflationary growth in 1994 and an acceleration in 1995 assume continuing budget consolidation. Fiscal slippage, by undermining business confidence and by reversing the downward interest-rate trend, would, likewise, have considerable adverse effects on growth, employment and inflation.

IV.   Structural unemployment
and labour market rigidities

The Spanish unemployment rate was low and below the average of OECD Europe and the OECD area as a whole until 1977. However, unemployment in Spain surged after 1977, and since 1985 its rate has been on average double that of OECD Europe. It is projected to reach almost 25 per cent in 1994, 3½ percentage points above its previous peak in 1985, and it is unlikely to decline significantly before 1996.[26] The high level and the trend increase in the unemployment rate for a country with one of the fastest GDP growth rates (3 per cent yearly) in the OECD since 1986 underscores the predominately structural nature of the problem.

This chapter reviews the principal employment and unemployment trends and analyses the structural factors both on the supply and demand sides contributing to the persistence of high unemployment. Some of these factors are demographic or related to the economic and social development process, and are likely to continue pushing unemployment up over the medium-term. However, there are also institutional and behavioural factors hampering employment creation which are in principle responsive to policy initiatives.[27] The recent surge in unemployment and the associated sizeable budgetary costs have made more evident the deleterious effects of rigidities on employment creation, sparking off a series of labour market reforms. Important reforms aimed at controlling the budget costs of unemployment and contributing to reduce labour market rigidities were introduced in 1992 and a new package of even more wide-ranging reforms was recently presented to Parliament. These reforms, and related structural policies, are discussed at the end of this chapter.

Labour market trends

Long-term labour market developments can be divided into three periods. Only short references will be made to the first period of rapid GDP growth and employment creation until about the mid-1970s. The second period is character-ised by sizeable job destruction and goes up to 1985. The third period starting in 1986, covers the current economic cycle (with an expansionary phase until 1990 and a contractionary one since 1991) and is examined in more detail.[28]

Labour demand and supply

From 3.7 per cent in 1975 and 11.5 per cent in 1980 the rate of unemploy-ment rose to 21.5 per cent in 1985 (Diagram 10). This dramatic increase was the result of massive lay-offs, notably in the first half of the 1980s. Spain was affected more than most OECD countries by the two oil shocks and the ensuing slower GDP growth in the OECD area because:[29]

i) contrary to most OECD countries, which had liberalised trade to a great extent before the first oil shock, Spanish industry, reflecting high protective barriers, had not adjusted, and was, therefore, badly pre-pared to face intense competition in the ensuing prolonged world-wide economic slack. Until the second half of the 1970s, productivity was low across the board due both to protection-induced inefficiencies and to the extended job security system which was a counterpart to the low wages imposed under the Franquist regime. Moreover, industry was dominated by heavy sectors (iron and steel, non-ferrous metals, ship-yards, etc.), with excess capacity world-wide, and by light traditional sectors (textiles, clothing, shoes, etc.), which have been facing intense competition from low-wage countries since the mid-1970s;

ii) following the restoration of democracy, the pent-up demand for rapid wage increases reinforced the inflationary spiral and, by squeezing profits further in a period of sluggish sales, accentuated the labour shake-out.

Indeed, in the period 1976-85 total employment shrank by 14 per cent, with non-farm private sector dependent employment declining by as much as 23 per cent (Table 14). This explains the small acceleration in the annual rate of growth of non-farm productivity to $3^{1}/_{2}$ per cent, despite the slowdown in the growth of non-

53

Diagram 10. **EMPLOYMENT AND UNEMPLOYMENT TRENDS**

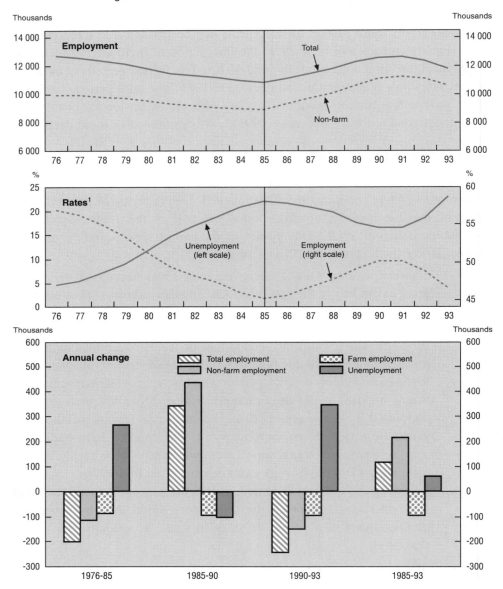

1. Unemployment as a percentage of labour force and employment as a percentage of population, both for age group 16-64 only.
Source: National Institute of Statistics and Ministry of Economy and Finance.

Table 14. **Civilian employment**

	1976	1980	1985	1990	1993	1992 Percentage share	1976-85	1985-90	1990-93
	Thousands						Annual percentage change		
Total civilian employment	12 704	11 797	10 870	12 579	11 805	100.0	-1.7	3.0	-2.1
By sex									
Male	8 960	8 362	7 700	8 576	7 829	66.9	-1.7	2.2	-3.0
Female	3 732	3 435	3 170	4 003	3 977	33.1	-1.8	4.8	-0.2
By sector									
Agriculture	2 775	2 259	1 975	1 485	1 196	10.1	-3.7	-5.5	-7.0
Non-agriculture	9 919	9 538	8 895	11 093	10 609	89.9	-1.2	4.5	-1.5
Industry	3 463	3 187	2 653	2 978	2 527	22.7	-2.9	2.3	-5.3
Construction	1 210	1 051	790	1 220	1 095	9.7	-4.6	9.1	-3.6
Services	5 246	5 299	5 451	6 895	6 989	57.5	0.4	4.8	0.5
By professional status									
Self-employed	2 367	2 254	2 253	2 115	2 032	16.7	-0.6	-1.3	-1.3
of which: in agriculture	1 151	973	883	687	575	4.8	-2.9	-4.9	-5.8
Family workers	1 191	1 046	876	684	536	4.6	-3.4	-7.8	-7.8
of which: in agriculture	673	526	435	291	216	1.8	-4.7	-7.7	-9.4
Employees, total	8 628	8 029	7 330	9 273	8 659	73.4	-1.8	4.8	-2.3
Agriculture	819	622	581	472	366	3.2	-3.7	-4.1	-8.1
Non-agriculture	7 809	7 407	6 749	8 801	8 292	70.2	-1.6	5.5	-2.0
Industry	3 040	2 811	2 308	2 628	2 187	19.6	-3.0	2.6	-5.9
Construction	1 018	844	558	963	813	7.3	-6.5	11.6	-5.5
Services	3 753	3 751	3 883	5 210	5 294	43.3	0.4	6.1	0.5
Public sector	1 286	1 454	1 736	2 106	2 109	17.5	3.4	3.9	0.1
of which: government	928	1 060	1 284	1 683	1 751	14.3	3.7	5.6	1.3
Private sector	7 342	6 575	5 594	7 167	6 550	55.9	-3.0	5.1	-3.0

Source: National Institute of Statistics and Ministry of Economy and Finance.

55

farm GDP to 1¾ per cent yearly from 6 per cent between 1965 and 1975. The cost-induced productivity gains were particularly important in industry (averaging 5½ per cent per year), where employment shrank 24 per cent.

Contrary to the job destruction in the period 1976-85, there has been considerable employment creation as a whole since 1986. Employment growth was very rapid (3.4 per cent per year) in the expansionary phase of the cycle until 1990, so that despite job losses since then, total employment grew by 1.1 per cent yearly between 1985 and 1993. However, this figure understates the positive job creation trends over this period. Reflecting its late industrialisation process, Spanish farm employment still accounted for 18¼ per cent of total employment in 1985 (*i.e.* three times higher than in the EC). The rapid transition towards a modern economy with high value-added industrial and services sectors and the associated improvement in the standard of living and in employment prospects since the mid-1980s reinforced the movement of labour out of agriculture. The rate of decline in farm employment stepped up to 6.2 per cent yearly between 1985 and 1993 from 3.7 per cent in the period 1976-85. As a result, the share of farm workers in total employment is now 10 per cent. In the period 1986-93, the destruction of 780 000 farm jobs (7 per cent of 1985 total employment) compares with the increase in unemployment of 550 000. However, it should be noted that even if such large agricultural job losses had not occurred, the unemployment rate on arithmetical calculations would still have been as high as 12 per cent in the peak of the economic cycle in 1990, and about 17 per cent in the 1993 trough, pointing to sizeable labour market disequilibria.

Non-farm employment creation appears impressive, with an average rate of growth of 4.5 per cent in the five years to 1990, and despite the decline in the following three, an annual increase of 2.3 per cent over the whole period (Diagram 11). This is twice as high as the OECD average and three times that of OECD Europe. Particularly rapid was the growth in government employment (3 per cent yearly in the period 1986-90), partly due to the regionalisation process. Non-farm private dependent employment also grew very fast (5 per cent yearly) during the upward phase of the cycle, with the strongest rates in construction (9 per cent) and in financial and related branches servicing companies (8½ per cent). The consequent slowdown in labour productivity growth, in particular non-farm business productivity, was very pronounced, from 3½ per cent yearly in the period 1981-85 to barely above ¼ per cent in the period

56

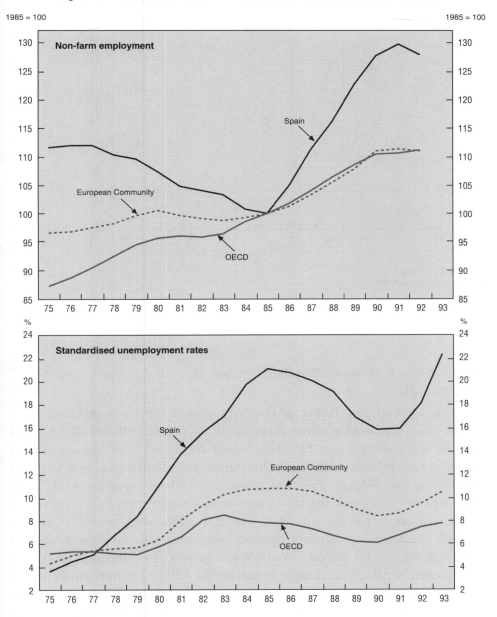

Diagram 11. **COMPARATIVE EMPLOYMENT AND UNEMPLOYMENT TRENDS**

1985 = 100

1985 = 100

Non-farm employment

Spain

European Community

OECD

Standardised unemployment rates

Spain

European Community

OECD

Source: OECD, *Labour Force Statistics* and *Main Economic Indicators.*

57

Diagram 12. **LABOUR PRODUCTIVITY GROWTH**

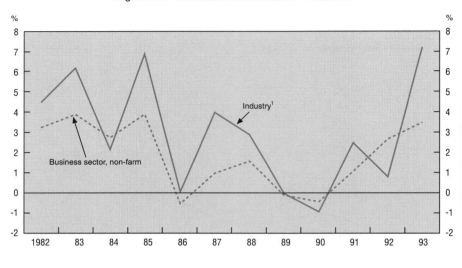

1. Excluding energy.
Source: OECD estimates.

1986-90, which is some two-thirds below that in the rest of the OECD (Diagram 12).

This atypical low labour productivity growth reflects a combination of factors. After the sizeable labour shake-out in the period 1976-85, labour hoarding had nearly disappeared by 1985, except for a very small labour surplus, mainly in sectors under industrial restructuring programmes (*e.g.* iron and steel, shipbuilding and mining). The virtual absence of labour overhang in 1985 contributed to the very quick and strong response of employment to the recovery in output growth, especially in 1986. Another explanatory factor is that in 1986-90 the main expansionary demand component was investment, with an annual growth of 11¾ per cent. And whereas prior to 1985 business investment was essentially capital deepening, in the period 1986-90 it was mainly capital widening (Diagram 13). Thus, the acceleration in the growth of capital stock over this period was associated with a small decline in the capital/labour ratio, and even including the subsequent rise, the growth in the ratio over the period

Diagram 13. **GROSS FIXED CAPITAL STOCK AND EMPLOYMENT**

1977-93 business sector, volume indices (1980 = 100)

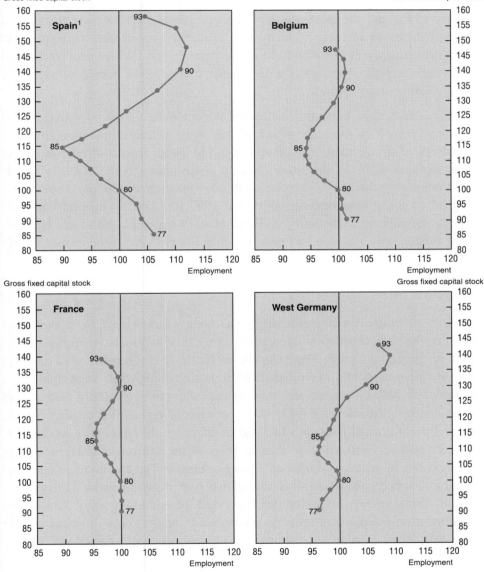

1. Non-farm employment.
Source: OECD estimates.

1985-93 was barely 1¼ per cent yearly compared with over 5 per cent in 1977-85. The capital widening bias, especially in the second half of the 1980s, is in part attributed to the improved economic outlook after joining the EC (in January 1986) and the relatively low level of labour costs, which encouraged domestic firms to increase capacity and attracted considerable foreign direct investment, mainly in greenfield sites. Furthermore, the Government introduced wide ranging employment promotion policies around 1984, which considerably boosted hirings (see below).

Sizeable net employment creation and the euphoria associated with the rapid economic growth of the second half of the 1980s detracted attention from the persistence of strong labour market rigidities and labour market disequilibria. But these surfaced with the downturn, largely contributing to the sizeable labour shake-out during the last three years. Non-farm business dependent employment declined by 8 per cent between 1991 and 1993 (the decline in total non-farm business employment amounting to 6 per cent). As a result, non-farm business sector productivity – which had risen by only 1½ per cent cumulatively during the upward phase of the cycle – increased by 7½ per cent in the period 1991-93. This counter-cyclical pattern of labour productivity compares with a more normal pro-cyclical pattern in most OECD countries.

Overall employment performance has been characterised by a swift and strong response to production fluctuations as cyclical factors have been superimposed on structural factors. The main causes for the strong sensitivity of employment to output are found in the factors responsible for high real wage rigidity (to be analyzed below), strong inflation inertia and more generally widespread labour market distortions. Furthermore, because of rigid rules concerning the distribution of normal hours worked and overtime work, total hours worked per week are also very inflexible, so that the brunt of the adjustment is borne neither by wages nor by hours worked, but by employment.[30] The employment response to output has been magnified since the second half of the 1980s by the introduction of employment promotion schemes and legislation greatly facilitating recruitment on a fixed-term basis, part-time work, and training of young people (Annex I). The advantage of temporary contracts was not confined only to the absence of high lay-off costs, but they also made it possible to circumvent the difficulties in moving workers both horizontally and vertically to keep abreast with technical change and managerial needs and to adjust manpower to market fluctuations over time. Upon their introduction in 1984 the "new" labour market measures had immediate success, and no doubt contributed to the reversal of the downward employment trend in the mid-1980s, at the first signs of the pick up in economic activity. In effect in 1985, the first full year when all the "new" measures were operative, there was a marked increase in total hiring, nearly all under temporary contracts (Diagram 14).[31] In 1993, temporary employees accounted for one-third of total employees, the highest level among OECD countries. Spain also has one of the highest and fastest rising labour turnover ratios in the OECD. Although there has been substitution of temporary for permanent employees, the mid-1980s reforms had a large positive net job creation effect, as underlined by the near stagnation in labour productivity and the strong stimulus it gave to the growth of the labour force.

Primarily because of the discouraged worker effect illustrated by a marked fall in the participation rate, civilian labour force growth was only ½ per cent yearly between 1976 and 1985, almost one-half below the rate in OECD Europe

Diagram 14. **NEW PLACEMENTS**

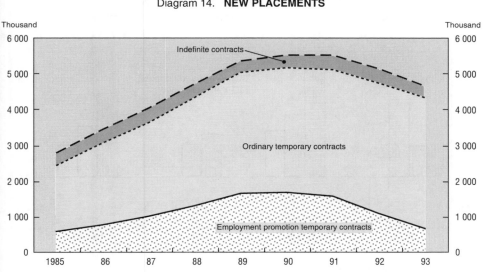

Source: Ministry of Labour and Social Affairs, *Boletín de Estadísticas Laborales.*

61

(Diagram 15). Between 1985 and 1993 the annual rate of growth of the civilian labour force rose to 1.3 per cent, surpassing that of OECD Europe and the OECD average by a wide margin, reflecting a somewhat faster growth in civilian working-age population and above all the swing to an increase in the participation rate (Diagram 16) – which nevertheless remains in 1993 among the lowest in OECD countries excluding Turkey.

Though at a slower pace than before, the male participation rate has continued to fall since 1985, reflecting a marked increase in school attendance, mainly in higher education, as well as early retirement. Though considerably less steep than for these two age groups, the participation rate of prime aged males (25-59) was also on a downward trend over this period and was cyclically sensitive. Contrary to the trend in male participation, the female participation rate, after remaining broadly flat at around 35 per cent between 1972 and 1985, reached 44 per cent in 1993. The trend-increase in the participation rate of prime aged females has been considerably stronger than the cyclical variations, so that even

Diagram 15. **LABOUR FORCE GROWTH**

Contribution of working age population[1] and participation rate

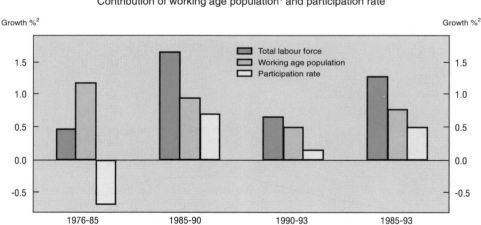

1. Civilian population aged 16 to 64 years old.
2. Average annual percentage change.
Source: National Institute of Statistics and Ministry of Economy and Finance.

Diagram 16. **PARTICIPATION RATES**

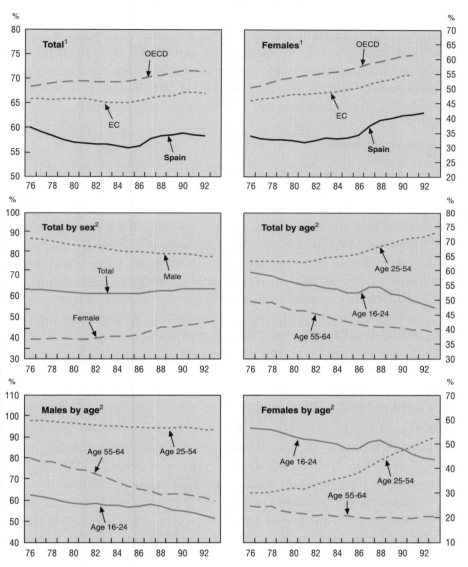

1. OECD data covering age group 15 to 64. The OECD total for females excludes Iceland and Turkey.
2. Spanish employment statistics covering age group 16 to 64.
Source: National Institute of Statistics, Ministry of Economy and Finance, and OECD *Labour Force Statistics*.

in the recent sharp downturn there was again a significant increase in their participation rate (5¼ percentage points over the last three years). This long-term upward trend in female participation, which is expected to continue, is explained by the social transformation in Spain of the mid-1970s, the marked fall in the birth rate and the expanding service sector in which women traditionally hold a large proportion of jobs. However, at 44 per cent, the female participation rate remains almost 10 percentage points below the European average.

Rising unemployment

The decline in demand for labour since 1991, combined with rapid growth in the non-farm labour force led to a record unemployment rate of 23¾ per cent at the end of 1993 from a cyclical low of 16¼ per cent in 1990. Registered unemployment rose at a slower pace to 17¼ per cent of the labour force at the end of 1993 from 15½ per cent in 1990.[32] Although it is generally accepted that Spain has a relatively large underground economy and that unemployment figures hide a certain number of workers either working or unwilling to work, there are no reliable estimates in this field. The comparison of unemployment rates in Spain and comparable European countries also reinforces the belief that Spanish unemployment figures overstate the true labour market slack. Moreover, the employment rate (*i.e.* employment as per cent of the working age population) gives a less dramatic picture of the deterioration of the labour market. It has dropped by 3¾ percentage points from its peak in 1990 but still remains 1 percentage point above the 1985 trough.

As expected in high unemployment countries where the job-search period for newcomers is very long, there is considerable youth unemployment (*i.e.* the 16-24 age group) in Spain (Diagram 17).[33] However, owing to the fall in the participation rate (due to longer studies), the near stable population of this age group and targeted labour market policies, the youth unemployment rate fell by one-fourth during the expansionary phase of the economic cycle and, despite the subsequent rise, it was only marginally above the 1985 peak in 1993. In contrast, though being much lower than the youth rate, the unemployment rate of the 25-54 age group did not fall much during the expansionary phase and exhibited a sharp cumulative increase after 1990, so that by 1993 it had significantly exceeded its previous peak. The rise in the unemployment rate of prime-aged males by 6 percentage points to 15½ per cent in 1993 was particularly rapid,

Diagram 17. **UNEMPLOYMENT PATTERNS**
As a percentage of labour force in each group

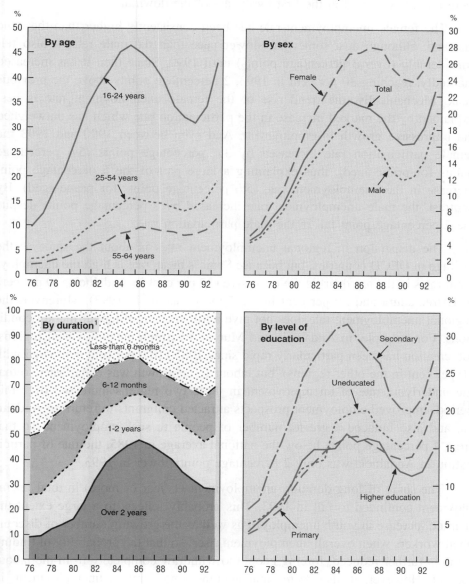

1. Per cent of total unemployment.
Source: National Institute of Statistics and Ministry of Economy and Finance.

indicating that the recession has also started to affect heads of households, who were relatively spared in the first two years of the downturn.

The female unemployment rate has been consistently higher than the male rate and, although at a somewhat slower pace than the male rate, it also fell considerably (over 3 percentage points) until 1990. Since then it has increased markedly, reaching 30 per cent in 1993, 2 percentage points above the previous peak. Mechanically, the trend rise of the female unemployment rate is best explained by the marked increase in the participation rate which has outweighed the impressive growth in employment. And even between 1990 and 1993 the female participation rate increased by $3\frac{1}{4}$ percentage points ($5\frac{1}{4}$ percentage points for prime-aged), thus explaining a large part of the 5 percentage point increase in the unemployment rate ($5\frac{1}{2}$ percentage points for prime-aged). By contrast, the male unemployment rate increased by 7 percentage points despite the 2 percentage point fall in the male participation rate.

The dispersion in regional unemployment rates is about the same as the average in OECD countries, but because Spain's mean rate is high the unemployment rates in the top quartile are excessive (32 per cent in Andalucia, 30 per cent in Extremadura and 29 per cent in the Canary Islands in 1993). Moreover, the regional unemployment rate does not give a full account of labour market conditions. For example, in Andalucia and Murcia, two high unemployment regions, job creation has been particularly rapid since 1985 ($16\frac{1}{2}$ per cent compared with 10 per cent in the other regions), but labour force growth was even faster so that the underlying rate of unemployment in these two regions increased over this period. Improved employment prospects attracted emigrants to return to Andalucia and also induced a greater number of people to seek employment, so that from 4 percentage points below the national average in 1985, the rate of participation in Andalucia was only 2 percentage points lower in 1993.

The share of long-duration unemployment (1 year or more) in total unemployment continued to fall in 1993. This probably reflects to a large extent the marked increase in youth unemployed as well as the growing number of discouraged workers when overall unemployment rises, so that the probability of finding a job is further reduced, forcing people to withdraw completely from the labour market. However, it also seems that genuine long-duration unemployment, in particular concerning male workers, has decreased compared with the first half of the 1980s, when there were sizeable job losses as well. Indeed, in contrast to this

Diagram 18. **STRUCTURAL UNEMPLOYMENT**

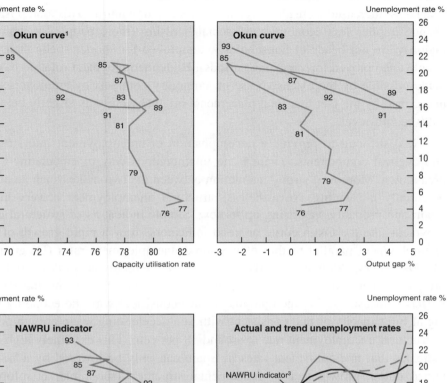

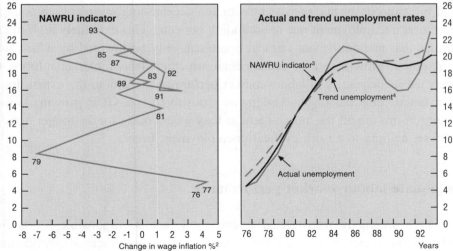

1. Mining and manufacturing.
2. Change in annual growth in private compensation per employee. Percentage points.
3. See OECD Economics Department working papers, No.132.
4. Obtained by Hodrick-Prescott filtering actual unemployment rates.
Source: OECD, *Main Economic Indicators* and OECD estimates.

earlier period, the number of people unemployed for shorter spells (less than one year) has increased considerably in the recent downturn. This compositional change implies less economic and social hardship (more people, of which the majority are not heads of households, unemployed for shorter spells than fewer people unemployed for very long periods). High unemployment rotation has been made possible by the extensive use of temporary contracts by employers and is underlined by the fact that total placements in 1993 were only slightly below the 1990 record level.

It is difficult to provide a decomposition of unemployment into structural and cyclical components. There is no unambiguous way of calculating such a breakdown. Moreover, strong interaction between the two makes such an attempt potentially misleading. Nevertheless, structural unemployment is very high in Spain and probably was rising up to now. Simple indicators of structural unemployment like the Okun curve or trend indicators show a rapid growth of trend unemployment parallel to that of measured unemployment rates (Diagram 18). The Okun curve, showing the trade off between unemployment rates and demand pressures, seems to have shifted up and become flatter since the mid-1980s.[34] Different measures like unemployment rates consistent with the economy working at full capacity or that consistent with non-accelerating wage growth point to a structural unemployment rate at around 18 per cent. This extremely high figure indicates that unemployment rates in Spain can only be lowered by a fast sustained output growth and by fundamental structural labour market reforms to correct the inadequacies in labour market performance. And, to the extent that a better functioning labour market impacts positively on GDP growth, labour market reforms are all the more urgent as they would make for a stronger upturn, therefore, helping to absorb cyclical unemployment faster.

Inadequate labour market performance

There are many inter-related fundamental factors responsible for labour market inefficiencies overall, and the Government has been increasingly addressing these issues in the last few years. The inadequate functioning is best illustrated by strong real and nominal wage rigidity (Table 15). Spain ranked up to now third among OECD countries in low responsiveness of nominal wage growth to unemployment rates and second in real wage rigidity.[35] Moreover, a

Table 15. **Real and nominal wage rigidity**

	Unemploy-ment rate [2]	Nominal wage elasticity with respect to [1]		Real wage rigidity		Sacrifice ratio [3]
		Prices short-run [4]	Unemploy-ment rate	Short-run	Long-run	
Spain	**13.5**	**0.25**	**-0.23**	**1.09**	**4.35**	**1.10**
	19	0.25	-0.17	1.47	5.88	1.52
United States	any	0.14	-0.61	0.23	1.64	1.23
Japan	1.9	0.66	-1.87	0.35	0.53	0.05
West Germany	3.6	0.75	-0.11	6.82	9.09	0.57
France	any	0.50	-0.29	1.72	3.45	0.43
United Kingdom	any	0.33	-0.15	2.20	6.67	1.65
Italy	7.2	0.60	-0.39	1.54	2.56	0.26
Canada	any	0.18	-0.51	0.35	1.96	0.98
Australia	any	0.50	-0.39	1.28	2.56	0.32
Austria	1.9	0.27	-0.87	0.31	1.15	0.29
Belgium	any	0.25	-0.25	1.00	4.00	1.50
Denmark	5.6	0.11	-0.31	0.35	2.10	0.87
Netherlands	6.5	0.50	-0.27	1.85	3.70	0.46
Sweden	1.9	0.25	-2.17	0.12	0.46	0.17
Switzerland	any	0.50	-0.28	1.79	3.57	0.45

1. Elasticities refer to the impact in the first half-year. Those for Spain and Denmark have been converted into semi-annual rates since data used for estimation is annual while semi-annual data was used for the rest of the countries.
2. For those countries with a non-linear Philips curve the elasticity with respect to the unemployment rate depends on the initial level of unemployment. In this case, the average unemployment rate in the estimation period is used in calculating the semi-elasticities. For Spain, the average unemployment rate for the period 1991-93 is used in addition to that of the estimation period.
3. Calculated as the mean lag of wages with respect to prices, divided by the annualised semi-elasticity of wages with respect to the unemployment rate.
4. All wage equations except the ones for Spain and Denmark are constrained to be homogeneous with respect to inflation in the long-run. The unrestricted equation estimated for Spain shows long-run homogeneity with respect to inflation, while that for Denmark rejects homogeneity reflecting some degree of money illusion.
Source: OECD.

non-linear relationship between wages and unemployment rates reflects a smaller wage responsiveness the higher the unemployment rates. Strong wage rigidity together with high inflation inertia provide a high sacrifice ratio. The cumulative percentage point years of unemployment required to reduce steady-state inflation by one percentage point is 1.5 in Spain, as compared with 1.2 in the United States or 0.1 in Japan. Neither nominal wages and prices nor real wages adjust sufficiently and quickly in the downturn. In order to keep the wage bill under control and thus ensure their viability, firms are obliged to shed labour massively when there is a cyclical or structural shock.

Wage/price and employment/output developments in the economic cycle 1986-93, in particular in the 1991-93 downturn, again highlight the strength of nominal and real wage rigidities. Since 1986 wage growth has acted as if the two sides in the collective negotiations had virtually the same implicit target year after year – a real increase of about 2 per cent – irrespective of labour market conditions and the prospects of the economy in general. According to wage surveys, the increase in non-farm business sector real wages has been about 2 per cent per year since 1985.[36] The weak cyclical response of real wages to employment conditions is best illustrated by the nearly 2 per cent increase in non-farm business sector real wages in 1993, *i.e.* after three years of virtual recession and in a year in which the unemployment rate jumped by almost 4 percentage points to nearly 23 per cent. In industry – the sector most exposed to foreign competition – wage growth was even higher. As real wages are fairly insensitive to the cycle, the brunt of the adjustment was borne by employment.

The rapid growth in the non-wage component of labour costs since the second half of the 1970s, after the change in the political regime, may also have contributed to wage rigidity. An approximate measure of the tax wedge for Spain and other selected OECD countries shows an average annual growth of just below 10 per cent in Spain for the period 1970-92, larger than that of the Netherlands (8 per cent), and much larger than France (3.5 per cent), or the United Kingdom (0.3 per cent). Wage claims might have been raised in order to compensate for the loss of an increasing part of earnings due to taxes. Since 1990 employee contributions have been broadly stabilised, but social security contributions paid by employers increased. This is reflected in an annual rate of growth of total compensation per employee since 1990 by about 1 percentage point per year faster than wage growth. As a result, the total tax wedge (*i.e.* the difference between real consumption wage and real labour cost paid by employers) continued to grow.

Wage bargaining and wage setting

A first explanation for the high degree of wage rigidity can be found in the semi-centralised wage bargaining and setting system. For the great majority of workers (6.5 million), wage negotiations are either on a sectoral or regional basis, and with a great deal of overlapping between the two.[37] The representatives of both sides in the negotiations, particularly those of employers, have traditionally been labour lawyers, mainly concerned with legal aspects and, influenced by the system's inertia, they tend to agree to roughly the same wage increases year after year, up to the point where marginal firms are driven to the verge of bankruptcy.[38] Moreover, for some sectors the agreement reached in one region is automatically extended to other regions. Because the pay norms established during the collective negotiations apply more or less uniformly to the regions and/or sectors concerned, the fixed component of the wage (mainly the basic wage, seniority and other fixed complements) is very large in Spain and, inversely the flexible component is small (between 10 and 15 per cent of the wage bill). This reduces the capacity of wages to absorb shocks so that the fall in employment is correspondingly sharper (Table 16). In addition, the agreed across-the-board wage rises are taken as a floor, with many firms tending to give bigger rises so that the system has a strong inflationary bias. The absence of downward wage flexibility penalises high unemployment regions. The regional differences in nominal wages are to a large extent offset by differences in price

Table 16. **Nominal value added and labour costs**[1]

Business sector

	$\dfrac{1990}{1985}$		$\dfrac{1992}{1990}$
	Average annual growth rate		
Nominal value added (at factor cost)	10.4		6.8
Total labour costs	9.6		9.8
of which:			
Average wage	9.2		8.8
Employment[2]	1.3		-1.4
Memorandum items:			
Real consumption wage	2.5		2.7
Net profits, average over the period,			
per cent of equity	7.3		2.2
	1986	1990	1992
Financial charges, per cent of value added	19.2	16.9	18.4

1. Based on a survey of private and public sector enterprises.
2. Excluding employment losses due to closure of firms.
Source: Bank of Spain, *Central de balances* (1992).

71

levels, so that the variability in real wages is relatively small, especially when compared to the wide divergences in unemployment rates (Diagram 19).

Public enterprises have also reinforced wage inflation. Despite the fact that public enterprises' wage levels are much higher than in the private sector and that

Diagram 19. **REGIONAL RELATIVE UNEMPLOYMENT AND WAGES**
1991, national average = 100

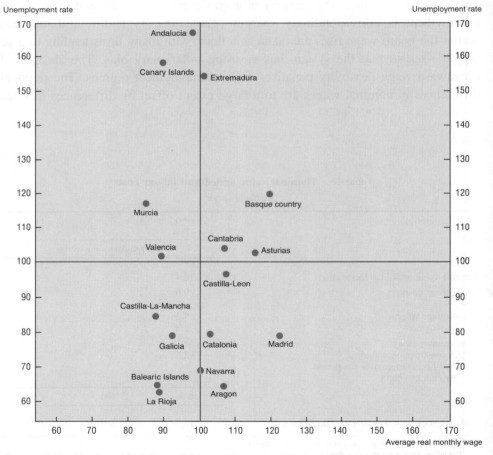

Source: National Institute of Statistics and Ministry of Economy and Finance, *Síntesis Mensual de Indicadores Económicos,* September 1992.

many of them are loss-makers, wage growth has been very fast in the last few years, exerting a strong pull on overall wage growth.[39] The apparent lack of wage discipline is related to the fact that these companies have been regularly bailed out and that dismissals are politically more difficult. Wage claims tend to be high, helped by the fact that unions are particularly strong in the public sector and managers do not show strong resistance to wage claims, knowing that there will be no sanctions. In order to cope with this problem and to impose greater discipline on public enterprises generally an inter-ministerial committee to monitor collective negotiations in public enterprises was set up last year.

Inflation inertia is also partly explained by the strong indexation elements in wage bargaining. Indexation was introduced during the period of high inflation in the 1970s to protect incomes from inflation spurts. At the beginning of the 1990s, although the official indexation mechanisms had long been repealed, 85 per cent of wage agreements in the private sector had indexation clauses, and in the public sector about 95 per cent. Indexation for central government employees was eliminated in 1993, but not in public sector enterprises.

In contrast, policies regarding minimum legal wages do not seem to have a large distorting influence in Spanish labour markets, contrary to the situation in many other European countries. The ratio of minimum to average wages has been on a downward trend during the 1980s and early 1990s, currently standing at 34 per cent (or 42 per cent of blue collar workers' average wage). Moreover, only 0.8 per cent of dependent employment in the non-farm business sector receives the legal minimum wage.

Labour market segmentation

An important source of rigidity derives from the excessive protection of permanent workers and low labour mobility. The tradition of job protection as a counterpart of low wage levels and insufficient unemployment insurance coverage has continued despite the sizeable growth in real wages and the generous unemployment coverage system put in place since the mid-1970s. Strict legal constraints regarding the dismissal of permanent workers puts serious restrictions on labour adjustment in periods of demand slack, resulting in many instances in the need for larger labour shake-outs once firms have approached bankruptcy situations due to prior unnecessary financial stress. Legal redundancy payments for permanent workers are considerably above those in most OECD countries,[40] thereby increasing employee resistance to wage moderation, even in the down-turn. Moreover, in order to avoid heavy bureaucratic procedures and industrial strife, employers and employees usually come to an agreement providing severance payments much higher than the legal levels, reaching 50 months salary on average. However, despite these high severance payments permanent employees are also dismissed, and not only in periods of slack. And this because total costs (including social security contributions) of hoarding permanent workers over the medium-term exceed severance payments.

Rigidities in managing permanent employees have been compensated to some extent by the introduction in the mid-1980s of temporary contracts with an automatic termination of the contract at the date of expiration accompanied by low redundancy payments.[41] This new scheme has been a major instrument for impressive net job creation in the second half of the 1980s. But fixed-term contracts have also introduced further distortions. Restrictions on the duration of temporary contracts (which have a maximum extension of three years) together with rigidities involved in hiring a permanent worker have induced large employment turnovers and probably increased frictional unemployment. Consequently costs have been large for the workers, the firms and the economy as a whole. Continuous shifting between jobs means that the individual cannot benefit from seniority and other income premia related to the length of the service, and skills are lost so that human capital and overall productivity suffers. Firms are prevented from building up human capital and increase their administrative expenses. High employment rotation makes fiscal and labour controls more difficult, resulting in a system which is more prone to fraud and abuse, entailing large budgetary costs as well as an overburdening of INEM. To sum up, the rapid expansion of temporary employment appears clearly as a second best to fully liberalising the labour market and led to the segmentation of the labour market, so that the increased flexibility in employment allowed by the temporary contracts was not reflected in wage behaviour.

Both functional and geographical mobility have traditionally been very difficult in Spain. With the aim of promoting corporatism in all spheres, the Franquist regime introduced the *Ordenanzas Laborales*, most of which are still operative. These rules, applying to different trades and sectors, strictly regulate workers' functions and establish demarcation lines, which impede both vertical and horizontal mobility. Only very few *Ordenanzas* have been repealed and replaced by flexible rules incorporated into new sectoral collective agreements (*e.g.* the one applying to the construction sector in 1992). Legal impediments exist to employers' transferring workers among factories in different geographical locations and, more generally, to any substantial changes in working conditions. According to current regulations, changes in working conditions must be discussed with workers' representatives and authorised by the labour administration. There is an administrative bias towards denying authorization unless there is previous agreement among workers and employers, which significantly raises the cost of the agreement.

Despite the wide differences in unemployment rates, inter-regional mobility in Spain has been low throughout the 1980s and early 1990s. Furthermore, some of the regions with the highest net immigration rates in the second half of the 1980s were those with the highest unemployment rates (*e.g.* Andalucia and Extremadura), while rich and low-unemployment regions, such as Madrid and Catalonia, had by far the highest net emigration rates between 1987 and 1991.[42] This atypical migration pattern is due to both economic and institutional factors. High unemployment benefits and income assistance over long periods weaken the incentive to move to another region. In particular, special rural programmes applied to farm workers in Andalucia and Extremadura have been an important incentive for people not only to stay in these regions but also for emigrants to return. This explains the much lower rate of decline in farm population and farm workers than in other regions since those schemes were set in place in the first half of the 1980s. High rents and property prices in expanding areas, because of restrictions on urban land, and heavy taxes on real estate transactions coupled with high home ownership (around 82 per cent) also discourage geographical mobility.[43]

High reservation wage

The generous unemployment coverage system put in place during the 1980s, in particular the extension of the duration of unemployment benefits and assistance in 1984 and 1989, has substantially raised reservation wages, thereby reducing effective labour supply and weakening downward pressure on wages. The system provides an incentive to certain population categories to change jobs often and receive unemployment benefits between two jobs. The sizeable severance payments also raise reservation wages by financing longer search time for unemployed workers.[44]

The unemployment replacement ratio for a typical worker is currently 70 per cent of the social security contribution base (approximately equal to wages at the time of contribution) during the first six months of unemployment and 60 per cent thereafter.[45] Because unemployment income support was exempt from both income taxes and social security contributions until January 1994, effective replacement rates may be much higher than nominal rates, so that for some wage categories net unemployment support is higher than the last net wage. The effective marginal tax rate (EMTR) gives a good illustration of existing incentives to remain unemployed with unemployment insurance payments rather than working.[46] Spain has a very high EMTR for all levels of gross income and above 100 per cent for very low income brackets (Diagram 20). The EMTR for the level of earnings of an average production worker (APW) is more than 80 per cent in Spain as compared with less than 60 per cent in Germany and below 40 per cent in the United States. More anomalously, for earnings somewhat above those of an APW, the EMTR rises to 90 per cent. Even for very high earnings, the EMTR remains above 70 per cent as compared with below 40 per cent in Germany and United States. Clearly the incentive to work is negative for very low paid jobs, and small for average-wage blue collar jobs. This helps to explain, first, the paradox often observed in recent years of serious shortages of low-skilled labour while extremely large unemployment rates persist; and, second, the rationality underlying the common practice by many workers (in particular when they are not heads of households) of periodically leaving employment to get unemployment benefits, especially during the second half of the 1980s when finding work was relatively easy.

INEM verifies the legal requirements needed to receive unemployment compensation and, in principle, monitors the unemployed throughout the duration of benefits. However, the controls, such as the periodical presence of persons receiving unemployment benefits and assistance in the offices of INEM, are not effective. The authorities are now thinking of crossing off the unemployment register those people refusing to take up the jobs offered to them by INEM. Moreover, there is anecdotal evidence that there is sometimes collusion between an employee not willing to take up a job offer and the employer, unwilling to employ someone who does not want to work and who therefore declares that the

Diagram 20. **EFFECTIVE MARGINAL TAX RATES (EMTR)**[1]

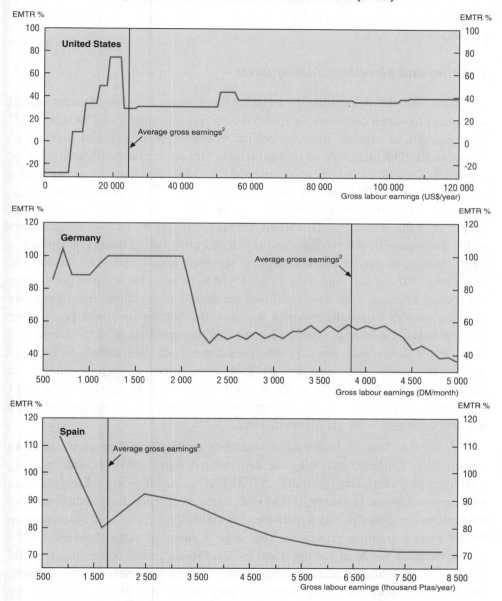

1. Data refer to a married worker with dependent spouse and two dependent children.
2. Gross earnings of an average production worker in 1992.
Source: OECD, *The Tax Benefit Position of Production Workers* (1993) and national authorities.

latter does not meet his requirements. Fraud in the unemployment field entails substantial budgetary costs, reduces incentives for work and contributes to keeping wages high.

Training and placement inadequacies

Although the dispersion in unemployment rates according to educational attainment has been considerably reduced with respect to the mid-1980s, it is still large enough to suggest an inappropriate matching of supply and demand of labour skills. The incidence of unemployment among workers with secondary or pre-university studies is 10 percentage points larger than among university graduates; and these medium-skilled workers account for 57 per cent of total unemployment.[47] This may be explained by serious mismatches between demand and supply of skills, as well as aspirations for higher wages by people with medium skills. To cope with this problem and also to improve labour quality in general, a large number of labour market training schemes were introduced around the mid-1980s. Young and long term unemployed have been the main target groups, but special schemes were also introduced for rural workers and to retrain workers in ailing sectors and self-employed workers. In addition to subsidies covering training costs, a generous system of grants accompanied most of the schemes.[48] However, it seems that many people joined these schemes mainly in order to receive the grants and subsidies attached, irrespective of their aptitudes and desire to acquire the specific skills. The efficiency in terms of skill building of these programmes seems to have been low overall and the grants and subsidies for new contracts were abolished in 1992.

A regular flow of information regarding employment opportunities is an essential tool for better matching the demand and supply of skills, and reducing total unemployment. Until recently, only INEM was legally entitled to operate as a placement agency. However, INEM is also responsible for the administration of unemployment benefits and assistance, for controlling fraud and for managing labour market training programs. The large number of tasks imposed on the institution have not been accompanied by a sufficient provision of resources. Its services as a job-finding and brokerage agency, which were never really efficient, suffered even more following the recent surge in the number of applicants for unemployment benefits. Another reason for its inefficiency is that INEM offices are regionally based, and there is no adequate flow of information regarding vacancies between regions. Placements handled directly by INEM usually represent 7 to 10 per cent of total hiring, by far the greatest percentage of hiring being done by firms themselves. In the last few years, private placement agencies emerged calling themselves consultancy firms, to circumvent the INEM's legal monopoly in the placement field.

Labour market reforms and the challenges of the 1990s

The rising trend in the female participation rate and the declining trend in farm employment are expected to persist, so that despite the projected marked deceleration in the growth in the working-age population, non-farm labour force growth is likely to be in the order of 1 per cent yearly over the medium term.[49] On this basis, labour supply is unlikely to provide any significant relief for the unemployment problem before the end of the century. At the same time GDP growth is unlikely to be as strong as during the second half of the 1980s (when it averaged $4^{1}/_{2}$ per cent per year), when it benefited from the stimulus provided by the entry into the EC and the associated increase in foreign investment. Coherent structural policies aimed at reducing labour market rigidities and easing labour cost pressures will be essential to generate a high rate of job creation, so that unemployment can start falling rapidly. Recognising the importance of the problem, the Spanish authorities have undertaken the reform of the labour market since 1992. They concentrated first on the reduction of budgetary costs of unemployment and then, more significantly, on the mechanisms underlying the functioning of the labour market.

Budgetary measures that reduce reservation wages

The beginning of the economic downturn in 1991 revealed the malfunctioning of the labour market and its adverse effects on unemployment, as well as the high budgetary costs of the social welfare system put in place during the 1980s. Some reform measures were introduced in 1992 in order to cope with an uncontrollable growth in transfer payments by 21 per cent between the first halves of 1991 and 1992 for unemployment benefits and sick leave payments. Eligibility for unemployment benefits was tightened, and payment and duration of benefits were reduced. Unemployment benefits were again lowered in December 1993 and, starting in January 1994, have become subject both to income taxes

79

and to social security contributions, while they were exempt before.[50] However, the tax regime remains more generous than for wage income.[51] All in all, reservation wages should have been significantly lowered by these measures.

As mentioned before, in 1992 grants and subsidies (including reductions in employers' social security contribution rates) given to the unemployed under different training schemes were discontinued in order to reduce abuses and lighten budgetary costs. At the same time, a subsidy of Ptas 550 000 was given for the conversion of on-the-job and vocational training contracts into permanent contracts. The elimination of subsidies for training led to a marked decline in new hiring under the training schemes, but only a small number of contracts were converted into permanent ones.[52] Social security deductions given for the employment of targeted groups were also discontinued.[53] The option given to the unemployed to take up the unemployment insurance payment in a single instalment in order to start a new business as a self-employed worker was abolished due to the poor results of this scheme and the high budgetary cost.[54] Finally, measures were taken to curb abuse of sick leave payments as a substitute for unemployment benefits.[55] In addition to the budgetary yield, the associated greater transparency and the fact that this category of unemployed people, previously unrecognised, now registered as unemployed, will contribute to improving the efficiency in the labour market.

Measures enhancing labour market flexibility

Beyond the above measures that were prompted by budget overruns, the Government, preoccupied by the sharp rise in unemployment, decided to introduce far-reaching labour market reforms aimed at lifting barriers to job creation. A decree was passed at the end of December 1993 and a draft law has been presented to Parliament and is expected to become law by the middle of 1994. The draft law significantly modifies the fundamental law *(Estatuto de los Trabajadores)* of 1980 regulating work and social security conditions.

Considerable emphasis is placed on facilitating the flexible allocation of labour resources. The rigid working hour limits adversely affecting both capital and labour productivity and overall production costs would be practically lifted, with the limit of a 40 hour week set as an annual average. This allows regular working schedules and an unequal distribution of working hours throughout the year following production fluctuations.[56] Working schedules would be set in sectoral/regional agreements but, according to the draft law, they would also be changed, when necessary, by agreement among employers and workers' representatives. This measure would greatly reduce the need for overtime and thereby considerably reduce labour costs. While maintaining the yearly 80 hour limit for overtime work, the minimum overtime pay rate would be brought down to the ordinary pay rate, whereas now the former is 75 per cent above the latter.

With the same aim, changes affecting working conditions would be made considerably easier, especially when these concern a relatively small number of workers.[57] Under the draft law, for changes affecting a small number of workers, employers would no longer need to consult workers' representatives and would no longer be obliged to notify the change to the Ministry of Labour. For changes affecting a large number of workers, workers' consultations and administrative authorization would still be required; but as regards the geographical transfer of a large number of workers, in case of disagreement the transfer should not be delayed by the administration for more than 6 months. Functional mobility, severely restricted by the *Ordenanzas Laborales*, would be facilitated for ''equivalent'' worker categories, *i.e.* those having similar qualifications. In addition, the draft law proposes the total phasing out of the *Ordenanzas Laborales* by end 1995 at the latest, and invites industrial partners to replace it with collective agreements regulating working conditions.

The draft law simplifies lay-off procedures. Dismissal of a small number of workers (treated as if they were individual dismissals) would no longer require prior consultation with workers' representatives and administrative authorization.[58] However, dismissed workers would have the right to appeal to labour courts. Collective lay-offs (as opposed to individual lay-offs) would still require consultation with workers' representatives and administrative authorization. But under the draft law, the administration will have 15 days to reply instead of the current 30 days, otherwise dismissals will automatically be approved, whereas at present no reply is taken as a refusal. In addition to the existing reasons for collective dismissals (technological, economic and major reasons, usually invoked when a firm sustained losses for two consecutive years) the draft law includes organisational and production reasons. These additional arguments should greatly facilitate dismissals when the economic situation requires it. Therefore, firms would not have to wait to incur losses for two years before lay-off proceedings begin. By then the firms' situations have often deteriorated so much that returning to a stable situation necessitates a considerably larger number of dismissals than if the adjustment was operated at an earlier stage. Legal redundancy payments remain untouched by the reform, but the effective cost (*i.e.* that agreed above legal provisions) should be markedly reduced, since in many instances it would no longer be necessary to secure employees' agreement.

As a counterpart to making dismissals of permanent employees easier and less costly, fixed-term contracts under the category of employment promotion schemes (*i.e.* those not justified by the content or temporary nature of the job) would be eliminated.[59] ''Ordinary'' fixed-term contracts, justified by the content of the task to be performed, which in fact account for almost two-thirds of temporary hiring, would remain.

All these measures would bear positively on wage bargaining and setting. But in order to increase the flexibility of the wage determination process further, the draft law envisages that firms in difficult economic situations may be exempted from implementing wage settlements fixed in regional or sectoral collective agreements. The Government also expects that deregulation would encourage firms to increase the variable component of the total wage bill, for example by making use of productivity and output-related premia. This would permit wages to directly absorb a larger part of cyclical shocks, so that employment is less affected.

In order to put pressure on industrial partners to revise collective negotiation procedures radically, the draft law would establish that new agreements would automatically cancel previous ones, except for those clauses and aspects that are expressly retained. In this way the negotiating parties would be forced to revise many important aspects of labour relations agreed to a long time ago, but which have become obsolete.

With the aim of facilitating the access of the young to the labour market, an apprenticeship contract was introduced in a December 1993 decree. It can be applied to workers aged 16-25, without post-secondary or higher education, for a duration of 6 to 36 months and with the remuneration set in the corresponding collective agreements, with a minimum of 70, 80 and 90 per cent of the minimum legal wage for the first, second and third years respectively.[60] And the social security contribution rates are also lower than those applying to fixed-term and indefinite contracts, reflecting the lack of coverage for unemployment and pensions. Many people have been recruited under the apprenticeship contracts since their introduction in December 1993 and the average wage is higher than the minimum stated in the law. Moreover, on-the-job training programs were modified, so that only people with post-secondary or higher education are eligible with the contract duration of 3-36 months being narrowed to 6-24 months. Remuneration, unless expressly set in collective agreements, will be at least 60 and 75 per cent for the first and second years respectively, of the wages set in collective agreements for a similar post.[61] Training and retraining for employed workers, which up to recently has not received much attention, is expected to become more efficient after transferring the management of programmes and funds to employers and unions. The transfer of the management is expected to be completed in a three year period which started in 1993.[62] Moreover, a National Programme for Professional Training covering the period 1993-96 was approved last year in order to improve coordination of the three basic training institutions, the Foundation for Vocational Training (FORCEM), the Ministry of Education and INEM. In line with the decentralisation process many of the training activities are being transferred to the Regions and the overall management will be exercised by FORCEM.

Labour market flexibility was also increased in the December 1993 decree by lifting all restrictions on the duration of part-time working.[63] It also made a first step towards the abolition of the job brokerage monopoly of the public employment service. Notifying INEM of vacancies which was a pure formality, is no longer required, although firms must continue to report hiring. The establishment of private placement agencies has become legal, though they are required to be non-profit making and to have prior INEM authorization; firms specialised in the temporary placement of workers are now legal and the rules governing them will be set in a forthcoming law.

Overall assessment

The reforms of the 1980s liberalised a segment of the labour market, which, combined with a considerable expansion of active labour market measures, gave a strong impetus to employment growth in the second half of the 1980s. At the same time, the scope and generosity of income support policies, especially for the unemployed, increased markedly. Public expenditure on passive labour market policies catering for the unemployed has averaged 2½ per cent of GDP since 1985. At the beginning of the downturn, the Government, preoccupied by the growing burden of the steeply rising unemployment benefits on public sector finances, reduced the generosity of the system somewhat. Pressed by the rapid increase in unemployment in 1992-93, the Government has now put emphasis on improving the functioning of the labour market overall. And recognising that selective measures dealing with partial aspects of the problem no longer suffice, and might even be counterproductive over the longer run, a broader approach is now envisaged.

Reform measures, once adopted, could have a significant impact on employment creation.[64] Important labour market rigidities would disappear and a good deal of dynamism would be gained in labour market relations by transferring the vast majority of aspects previously contained in the law into collective agreements. However, the draft law does not address the high level of legal severance payments and certain aspects of wage determination. There is also the risk that social partners may not reach agreement, at least at the beginning, and the consequences of this are difficult to predict. Another question that might be raised is whether the liberal measures regarding changes in working conditions and lay-offs will be well accepted and whether employers and unions will change their behaviour accordingly. If a great number of decisions are challenged and labour courts are called to arbitrate, it is essential that labour courts stick to the spirit and the letter of the law, and do not adopt the labour administration's protectionist attitude towards workers.

The tightening of the social welfare system, in addition to helping redress budget imbalances, will also reduce reservation wages, and have a long term moderating impact on wage growth, further favouring employment creation. Because of the timing of the measures, they might have a pro-cyclical effect of accentuating the down-side of the cycle in the short run, but this should be quickly more than compensated for by the pervasive beneficial effects of the labour market reforms.

Reforms in training policies are progressing in the right direction. Apprenticeship contracts may largely help to smooth the link between school and the job market for young workers, up until now a very difficult passage. On the other hand, guarantees of control regarding the training content of apprenticeship and on-the-job training contracts are too loose. A serious effort is needed to prevent these type of contracts from becoming a means of hiring cheap labour. Lack of monitoring may result in extremely high job rotation among the young without any success in helping to establish them in the labour market.

V. Conclusions

In the five years to 1990 the Spanish economy was characterised by a broad and strong expansion. EC entry, stimulating a marked increase in foreign direct investment and modernisation efforts by domestic producers, led to a very fast growth of investment (nearly three times the OECD average). Reinforced by lax fiscal policy and high wage rises consumption also expanded rapidly, so that domestic demand growth reached the unsustainably high rate of 7 per cent per year over this period. These developments were superimposed on an already inflation-prone economy, producing serious macroeconomic imbalances. When the cyclical downturn began in 1991 domestic inflation had risen to over 7 per cent, the current balance of payments deficit to $3^{1}/_{4}$ per cent of GDP, the structural budget deficit to over 6 per cent of GDP and, despite an unemployment rate of 16 per cent, labour hoarding had increased, squeezing profit margins.

The adjustment process since 1992 has, therefore, been particularly forceful, resulting in a marked increase in the unemployment rate to 24 per cent at the end of 1993. Reflecting a rapid deterioration in business and household confidence, domestic demand fell by $3^{1}/_{2}$ per cent in 1993. The slack and the devaluations of 1992 and 1993 made possible a shift of resources to the external sector, limiting the fall of GDP to 1 per cent and leading to a sharp decline in the current external deficit to $^{3}/_{4}$ per cent of GDP in 1993. Consumer price-inflation also fell somewhat, but at nearly 5 per cent it remained considerably above the OECD average, while the budget deficit doubled to $7^{1}/_{4}$ per cent of GDP.

Better balanced policies, the enactment of structural reforms and the upturn in OECD Europe suggest more favourable macroeconomic conditions in the period ahead. According to OECD projections, GDP growth is expected to be slightly above 1 per cent in 1994. The earlier years' high wage rises and interest rates as well as the need to address the accumulated fiscal drift will continue to be a serious drag on GDP; in particular, private investment is projected to decline further. Influenced by the unemployment trend, and in line with recent settlements, wage growth is expected to slow and the 12-month increase in consumer prices may fall to 3¾ per cent at the end of 1994. If the disinflation momentum is maintained, GDP growth could accelerate to 2¾ per cent in 1995, but this will in itself make only a small dent in the high unemployment rate of around 24½ per cent and only a limited reduction in the budget deficit is foreseen.

In view of the size of the problems facing the Spanish economy and because macro and micro policies reinforce each other, a two-pronged attack on macro-economic disequilibria and structural distortions is necessary to produce substantive results. Fiscal policy was recently tightened, and together with the effects of earlier measures, this may just stabilise the general government deficit at the high level of about 7 per cent of GDP in 1994 and the debt/GDP ratio is set to increase to 60 per cent. Moreover, the execution of the budget has proven difficult in the past, and rules and practices to keep spending in line with budget appropriations need to be strengthened if the sizeable budgeted cuts are to be realised. Abuse and fraud in the social security system also call for considerable tightening of controls, so as to avoid spending overruns in this area. Likewise, tax avoidance and evasion could also be curbed if new technologies for cross-checking income sources and payments, more frequent controls and speedier procedures against fraud were introduced.

It is essential to implement in full the 1994 Budget, but this is only a first step towards fiscal consolidation, and greater efforts will have to be made in order to meet the criteria set out in the Maastricht Treaty. A number of the 1994 measures, such as the wage freeze, cuts in non-wage consumption and the shift in pension indexation from past to anticipated inflation will help, but have only one-off effects on the budget deficit. In addition to the need to set up efficient control and enforcement mechanisms, the emphasis should be placed on containing outlays on a permanent basis. There is much scope for moderating the steep trend-rise in spending on pensions and health, and a public debate on possible solutions may prove extremely useful. The decision to replace only one out of two people leaving the civil service should be strictly adhered to and prolonged, so that the reduction of overstaffing in many government activities, which began last year, should continue. The rapid growth in spending by Regions and local authorities has also been responsible for budget overruns in the past and should, therefore, also be better controlled.

Financing the losses of public controlled firms is also a major cause for the budget drift. Many firms, knowing that they will be bailed out, do not make the necessary efforts to improve efficiency and increase financial discipline, as illustrated by the relatively high wage increases in public enterprises in the recent downturn. Tighter policies *vis-à-vis* these firms, including sanctions for management, would make them more efficient and able to withstand competition and also help to strengthen the public finances. Privatisation, as demonstrated in other OECD countries, would help to achieve both goals. The policy followed by the Government of making the capital of state monopolies available to private shareholders reduces the budget deficit but it does not fundamentally address the problem of efficiency. Speeding up privatisation should, therefore, be encouraged, as well as the contracting-out of certain projects. The Government is considering the latter approach in order to continue improving infrastructure without aggravating the deficit.

A faster reduction in the budget deficit than presently envisaged would also increase the credibility of the anti-inflation policy. Until recently, monetary policy bore the brunt of the anti-inflation effort. But, as it was not accompanied by appropriate fiscal and structural measures, its restraining effect on wage growth was very small, so that the frail fundamentals persisted and the devaluation of the peseta was not avoided, despite very high interest rates up to mid-1993. Interest rates subsequently declined markedly, leading to a substantial narrowing in the interest differential with Spain's ERM partners. Although there may be pressures for further cuts to strengthen the pace of recovery, it would not be prudent to undertake them until important progress is made in reducing the budget deficit and inflation. The Bank of Spain is expected to become independent later in 1994, strengthening credibility further.

The unemployment situation is the most critical economic problem in Spain. On the basis of past trends, even if GDP grows by about 3 per cent yearly in the second half of the 1990s, employment creation will be only a little faster than labour force growth, so that the fall in unemployment may be small. There are widespread labour market rigidities hampering employment creation in Spain. These, together with inflation stickiness, especially in services, are largely responsible for the very high structural unemployment. Rising unemployment benefits and the growing unemployment coverage since the mid-1980s have increased the reservation wage considerably. The Franquist regime's corporatist labour regulations, the *Ordenanzas Laborales* (fixing strict demarcation lines between skills and between crafts) are still alive and considerably impede functional and geographical labour mobility. Procedural hindrances in favour of job protection, even in cases where firms incur losses, make laying-off of permanent workers extremely difficult and costly, thereby discouraging the hiring of this category of workers. The extensive job protection legislation might have been socially justified when workers' wages and unemployment coverage were extremely low under the Franquist regime but, following the considerable rise in the social welfare coverage, this is no longer the case.

Around the mid-1980s, in order to circumvent these rigidities, the Government lifted impediments for temporary contracts; and almost all of the impressive growth in private sector dependent employment of the second half of the 1980s is accounted for by such contracts. However, to the extent that this has not been accompanied by a significant easing of lay-off rules for permanent workers, this is a second best solution, as it has led to a dual labour market: one part consisting of heavily protected permanent workers and the other of temporary workers with little protection. This segmentation aggravates the insider/outsider problem, thereby reinforcing the downward wage rigidity. Furthermore, the fast rotation of temporary workers increases costs and lowers overall productivity, as well as increasing frictional unemployment. Wages are very inflexible in Spain, which means that employment usually bears a disproportionate part of the adjustment burden, as again highlighted by the simultaneous strong growth of wages (nominal and real) and rapidly rising unemployment in the 1992-93 downturn.

Since 1992 the Government has started to introduce labour market reforms, to begin with mainly motivated by budgetary considerations. In 1992 the level of unemployment benefits and the duration of benefits in relation to the qualifying period were considerably reduced; part of social security sick leave payments were shifted to employers; and subsidies to training schemes with low efficiency were abolished. Despite these measures, net benefits for many categories of workers continued to exceed the net wage, so that the Government decided that unemployment benefits will be subject to income tax and social security contributions as from 1994, thereby further lowering the reservation wage.

In addition to these measures, the Government has presented a draft law modifying existing labour legislation significantly which at the time of writing is proceeding through Parliament. This draft law breaks with the corporatist philosophy of past legislation and is expected to increase labour market flexibility considerably. Lay-offs of permanent employees will be made much easier, notably by abolishing in many cases the requirement of administrative authorization. As a counterpart to this easing, temporary contracts for jobs of indeterminate duration will be abolished, but for specific duration projects, in which most temporary workers are employed, they will be maintained. Although it will affect a relatively small number of workers, this tightening goes against the trend of deregulation in Spain and creates disincentives to hire people. In order to limit this risk and to improve the quality of the workforce, a new apprenticeship scheme for young workers was introduced with correspondingly lower wages than for experienced workers.

In order to increase plant flexibility, significant changes in the regulations covering ordinary weekly hours and overtime pay will be introduced, so that work schedules correspond better to the fluctuations of demand and there is less resort to overtime work. The draft law also attacks the causes impeding horizontal, vertical and geographical mobility. The *Ordenanzas Laborales* will be repealed and replaced by collective agreements negotiated freely by industrial partners, who know better the specificities in each area. All in all, the proposed reforms are far-reaching, even though they do not address all the impediments to a better functioning of the labour market.

These measures are expected to start having a bearing on wage settlements, so that with time wage flexibility should also increase, even though the measures do not deal with the full range of factors which make the wage bargaining system rigid. However, the unemployment situation is already so critical, that it would be unfortunate if the labour market reforms are not associated with immediate wage moderation. The 1993 developments showed again the strong direct linkage between wages and unemployment, and only rapid progress toward the low rates of increase in wages of the best OECD performers would prevent another jump in unemployment, and help consolidate the recent gains in external competitiveness. By freezing wages of public servants the Government led the way in 1994; but unless private wage settlements fall markedly from the high 1993 levels of $5\frac{1}{2}$ per cent it will be difficult to maintain the disinflation momentum.

The Government's thrust on labour market reforms may explain the hesitancy in other fields, where there is also urgent need of deregulation. In the area of professional services and certain crafts big efficiency gains can be achieved and lower prices can be obtained if there is greater competition. However, progress in this area has been very slight overall, despite the recommendations of the Competition Court in its 1992 Report and the government's plans for passing appropriate legislation rapidly. State monopolies are another area where deregulation can produce sizeable benefits. However, except for allowing somewhat greater competition in the transport field, there has not been any significant change. Moreover, the monopoly of Telefonica in telecommunications (except for value added services which were liberalised in 1992), has been extended from 1997-98 (which is the limit for most EC countries) to 2002. Users will, therefore, not benefit immediately from better services and lower charges. Lastly, proposed legislation giving the possibility to Regions to restrict the currently relatively relaxed shopping hours also goes against the general trend of deregulation, and is likely to introduce distortions and increase further the inflation rigidities in the service sector.

In summary, faced with a high budget deficit and high and rising unemployment the Government has tightened its fiscal policy stance and has embarked on wide ranging structural labour market reforms. It is essential that announced policies be fully adhered to, even in the present difficult cyclical phase. Indeed, in order to meet the Maastricht Treaty's criteria even more courageous fiscal. policies are needed. A reform of selected social schemes, so as to concentrate benefits on the really needy, would contribute to stemming the rising trend in government spending. Efforts to bring inflation down to the rate of Spain's main EC partners must also intensify, and for this wage disinflation is the key and depends on the recognition by all concerned of the strong negative relationship between wage rises and employment growth. The Government can also contribute by introducing more competition in professional services and public utilities, the absence of which has been an important cause of inflation stickiness in this sector. The proposed labour legislation is a landmark for Spain and, if adopted, will increase labour market flexibility markedly. This, in conjunction with a more balanced policy stance, would reinforce confidence and lay the ground for the restoration of a sustainable growth path and strong job creation.

Notes and references

1. Symmetrically to the expansionary phase, the 1993 contraction in private consumption was essentially due to the sizeable drop in motor-cycle and private car registrations (50 per cent and 23 per cent respectively), and in purchases of durables, as indicated by the 12 per cent drop in department stores and super-markets' sales of non-food goods.

2. In Madrid, where house prices are the highest, the fall was 4.4 per cent; in Barcelona, ranking just below Madrid, house prices rose by 0.8 per cent; and in Malaga, a tourist region, they fell by over 10 per cent in 1993.

3. The profit share data have been derived from a sample of firms (roughly 6 000) covered by a survey and published by the Bank of Spain *Central de Balances, resultados de las empresas no financieras* (1992).

4. In many sectors, such as textiles, metal products, and machinery, lay-offs amounted to around 15 per cent of the labour force.

5. Multi-annual agreements usually project the high 12-month inflation at the moment of signing into the future, so that wage rises covered by the agreement are also high. They also include indexation clauses providing for real wage increases. Thereby, the greater the number of these agreements the more difficult disinflation becomes.

6. After the abolition of custom controls in January 1993, a new trade reporting system was introduced based on estimates made by individual firms, which circulate the relevant reports to the administration with a slight delay. This new system seems to have faced great difficulties, at least during the major part of 1993. Accordingly, the trade value data are subject to a larger margin of error than in the past. Even greater is the uncertainty regarding the split between prices and volumes. The figures in the text and tables should be taken as indicative of the order of magnitude involved and not to purport to measure precise price and volume changes. This also explains the small differences between customs and national accounts data.

7. Consumer price inflation in 1992 was boosted somewhat by indirect tax increases, so that the underlying improvement during 1993 is somewhat smaller than indicated by the above figures.

8. The inflation gap between services and industrial goods narrowed to $2\frac{3}{4}$ percentage points at the end of 1993, *i.e.* almost one-half the average gap between 1986 and 1992. The forces making for the wide inflation gap were analyzed in the *OECD Economic Survey of Spain, 1991/1992*, (Part IV).

9. In 1993 agreements were reached with the pharmaceutical industry and pharmacies to limit overall price rises to 3 per cent and to cut profit margins of pharmacies. Some 850 medicines were withdrawn from the list of products financed by the National Health System, thus putting additional pressure for price restraint.

10. It seems that the new trade reporting system understates the level of imports in 1993. Furthermore, because of speculative transactions and the anticipation of continuing strong growth in domestic demand, imports were very high in 1992, also underlined by the high rate of stockbuilding in 1992, so that the 1993 low import level incorporates an element of correction.

11. The cyclical dampening impact on revenues seems to have been relatively small, as the steeper fall in employment than had been assumed in the budget was largely offset by a steeper rise in nominal incomes.

12. The decline is smaller than budgeted, mainly because of continuing abuse, though this was probably less than before. There are reports that after the 1992 measures there are fewer people benefiting from sick leave pay, but for longer periods.

13. For a detailed analysis of the regionalisation process in Spain and the impact on public finances see the *OECD Economic Survey of Spain, 1992/1993* (Part IV).

14. The general government deficit on a cash basis was about $8^{1}/_{4}$ per cent of GDP. This difference is almost exclusively due to the extraordinary payments of nearly 1 per cent by INEM to cover the unemployment deficit pertaining to earlier years.

15. Treasury notes *(Pagarés del Tesoro)*, with a 5.5 per cent interest rate, used as a tax amnesty instrument, were completely phased out in 1993.

16. Interest payments are forecast to rise to $4^{1}/_{2}$ per cent of GDP, first, because payments in 1994 are still made on the basis of the high interest rates of 1992 and 1993, and, second, because of the rapidly shrinking share of non-interest bearing Bank of Spain loans and the elimination of low interest bearing Treasury notes coupled with the rapidly rising stock of debt.

17. First, three Regions which voted against this reform have the option to continue with the old financing system; second, three other Regions will not be allowed to apply this system until all "regional" responsibilities have been transferred to them; third, this percentage will be a component of the Region's participation in the State's tax receipts, so that the extra funds accruing to the richer Regions will not be so high as to undermine the global regional financing system; and, fourth, in order to make the transition smooth, temporary ceilings have been fixed limiting the growth of the extra revenues accruing to the individual Regions.

18. The "Special Unit Against Tax Fraud" has presented a report on methods for combatting tax evasion and will be given greater powers. The report places emphasis on improved information flows and better coordination between tax authorities at the different levels of government (State, Social Security, Regions and Municipalities), the use of computer technology for cross-checking declarations; and more in-depth controls and redefinitions of tax fraud, as well as sanctions, the severity of which will depend on the type of fraud.

19. The decline in interest rates was anticipated by markets, as underlined by the strong demand for bonds in the first part of 1993.

20. However, because of the sluggish response of commercial interest rates to changes in official rates and the big margin between deposit and lending rates, commercial lending rates may fall somewhat further in the course of 1994, even if inflation and interest rates in Spain's main EMS partners do not fall.

21. See: *OECD Economic Survey of Spain, 1991/1992* (Part IV), and *OECD Economic Survey of Spain, 1992/1993* (Part II).

22. The most important decisions for anti-competitive practices concerned: car dealers' agreements on price fixing for repair work and second-hand cars; the National League of Professional Football for abusing its dominant position in awarding exclusive broadcasting rights to a few television stations, and resulting in a fine of Ptas 147 million; six major banks for declaring similar maximum fees for certain services; and Telefonica (the State monopoly in telecommunications) for abusing its dominant position in tying up a leasing contract with the purchase of the equipment for lease.

23. For example, concerning dentists, approval by existing dentists operating nearby is required for a dental clinic to be set up, the practice of the profession is allowed only within the regional limits (and no further than 50 km outside the province of membership) and minimum prices are fixed by the association, so as to ensure a reasonable income for inefficient dentists. But anti-competitive rules, resulting in very high fees and, hence, ensuring sizeable rents to their members, is common in other professions (doctors, lawyers, architects, notaries and undertakers).

24. Wage settlements concluded in the first quarter of 1994 provided for an average wage rise of 4.2 per cent, composed of an increase of 4.3 per cent under previous years' multi-annual settlements and 3.2 per cent for new settlements.

25. The much lower 12-month consumer-price inflation to end-1994 than the average inflation in 1994 as a whole, reflects the exceptionally high food price levels at the end of 1993 and the markedly weaker effects of the 1992 and 1993 devaluations on consumer prices towards the end of 1994.

26. In Part IV working-age population, labour force, employment and the corresponding rates (*e.g.* participation and unemployment rates) include age groups 16-64 and therefore, there are slight differences with the data shown in the *OECD Labour Force Statistics* and the Spanish publications, which also include the age group of 65 years and over.

27. Some of these factors contributing to the strong labour market rigidities in Spain have been reviewed in Part II of the *OECD Survey of Spain, 1990/1991*; Part IV of the *OECD Survey of Spain, 1991/1992*; and Part V of the *OECD Survey of Spain, 1992/1993*.

28. The previous cycle ended in 1985, when the negative output gap (in relation to GDP trend) was $2\frac{1}{2}$ per cent and the unemployment rate $21\frac{1}{2}$ per cent. In 1986 a new ten year cycle started. It peaked in 1990, with a positive output gap of $4\frac{1}{2}$ per cent and an unemployment rate of $16\frac{1}{4}$ per cent. The downturn started in 1991. The trough seems to have been reached at the second half of 1993, but as the recovery phase appears to be weak, the negative output gap is projected to continue rising until 1995, when it is expected to reach $4\frac{1}{2}$ per cent with the unemployment rate at just over 24 per cent.

29. For a detailed analysis of labour market developments until 1985, see Part III of the *OECD Economic Survey of Spain, 1986*.

30. OECD econometric studies show that Spain has by far the highest cyclical elasticity of employment with respect to output in the OECD (Spain's elasticity is 0.85, followed by Australia with 0.79, as compared with 0.48 for Total OECD). The elasticity is calculated by estimating the trend deviations of employment with respect to trend deviations of real GDP for the period 1970-91, as reported in the study: *Unemployment and Labour Force Participation-Trends and Cycles*, by Jørgen Elmeskov and Karl Pichelann, Working Paper No. 130, Economics Department, OECD (1993).

31. The introduction of fixed-term contracts with no restrictions was aimed at promoting employment so that, although no special economic incentives were attached to them, they were identified as contracts under Employment Promotion Programmes (EPP). "Ordinary" fixed-term contracts justified by the temporal nature of the task already existed before and continued thereafter alongside those under EPP. Following the introduction of the EPP, controls on the "ordinary" contracts to assure that people hired were really employed for specific tasks and for limited duration were greatly relaxed, so that there have been considerably more hirings with "ordinary" fixed-term contracts than with EPP contracts.

32. Standardised (EPA survey) and registered unemployment in INEM show a peculiar pattern in Spain. Standardised unemployment is above registered unemployment when unemployment is on the rise and they converge when it declines. The gap between EPA and registered unemployment rates was 2 percentage points in the first half of the 1980s but it widened to 6½ percentage points at the end of 1993. There is much uncertainty regarding the reasons behind the gap and which is the most accurate measure of unemployment. The INEM usually registers people entitled to receive unemployment benefits, so that school leavers and people having exhausted unemployment benefit rights do not have an incentive to register, all the more so that INEM is a fairly inefficient placement agency. On the other hand, it seems that not all of the people reporting themselves as unemployed in the EPA Surveys are actually active job seekers, largely because they are cheaply employed in the underground economy.

33. Since 1985 the average job-search period of people without previous work experience is between 1 and 2 years for more than 20 per cent and more than 2 years for 50 per cent.

34. Two different measures are presented of the Okun curve with two different measures of output fluctuations, capacity utilisation rates and the output gap. The shifting of the curve is more clearly seen when measuring demand pressure with the output gap. This may be partly due to problems in measurement of the capacity utilisation rate. It comes from an opinion survey and the resulting figures are not very reliable.

35. Real wage rigidity, as measured here, reflects the cost in terms of a rise in the unemployment rate (6 percentage points over the long-run) in order to prevent real wages from increasing after a real shock. See: "Nominal Wages, the NAIRU and wage flexibility", by David T. Coe, *OECD Economic Studies No. 5* (1985).

36. Average wages derived from national accounts differ from those derived by business surveys because of methodological differences and shifts in the composition of the workforce, following the rapid growth in "low paid" temporary and other employees under the Employment Promotion Programmes.

37. For 1.1 million workers mainly in large firms wage bargaining and negotiations on labour conditions are on the firm level, so that first, there are permanent contacts between both sides, and second, the firm's profit/loss situation carries some weight in the negotiations.

38. The key role of lawyers in wage negotiations is the legacy of the Franquist period, during which wage rises were often imposed from above, so that the negotiators were essentially preoccupied with the legal technicalities of the agreement. As a result they paid less attention to the fundamental economic/financial problems and the conjunctural situation of the sectors and firms they represent.

39. Compared with the private sector as a whole, total earnings per hour worked in publicly owned coal mining firms (with sizeable recurrent losses) and in oil refineries are double, in electricity generating and distribution firms 70 per cent higher, in the tobacco industry 50 per cent and in the subsidised shipbuilding firms 30 per cent.

40. Legal redundancy payments for justified lay-offs are 20 days per year worked with a maximum of 12 months, but lay-offs found unjustified require either hiring back or compensation of 45 days per year worked with a maximum of 42 months. In practice, unless a previous agreement is reached between the worker or his representatives and the employer, all lay-offs are considered by labour authorities as unjustified, thus the corresponding compensation sets the minimum for settlements between workers and employees. According to employers, average redundancy payments are currently around 56 days per year worked.

41. 12 days per year worked.

42. See: *Regional Migration in Spain*, by Pablo Antolin and Olympia Bove, Documento de trabajo No. 9318, Bank of Spain (1993).

43. In addition, many people having a lease before the 1985 law, which partly liberalised new leases and rents, pay extremely low (regulated) rents. Since they cannot be evicted, they have no interest in moving out and taking a new higher lease. Moreover, rights on the old lease may be passed on to descendants.

44. The reservation wage is the wage which will induce an unemployed person to take up a job. The higher was his last wage and the higher are the unemployment benefits and other income related to his dismissals (*e.g.* severance payments) the higher is the reservation wage. The higher the reservation wage the longer a person is likely to be unemployed before he is ready to take up a job, especially if it is a lower paid job than his previous one.

45. The duration of insurance benefits is one third of the contribution period with a maximum of 24 months and a minimum qualifying period of 1 year. Upon expiration of unemployment insurance, the unemployed with family charges are eligible for unemployment assistance, which is 75 per cent of the minimum legal wage for varying periods of time (in some cases indefinitely) depending on family conditions. Unemployment assistance is also given to the unemployed with a minimum contribution period of 3 months. These provisions were considerably more generous before April 1992, when the level of insurance was 80 per cent, falling to 70 per cent of the contribution base and the duration of benefits in relation to qualifying time was much longer.

46. The EMTR includes not only marginal rates from the fiscal and social security systems but also has foregone opportunities for different forms of income and social support. However,

some caution is needed in cross-country comparisons because support measures other than income may not be homogeneously measured for all countries.

47.   The high unemployment rate of people with secondary education is partly explained by the large number of university students registering as unemployed, with the hope of finding a job immediately upon the end of their studies.

48.   Subsidies equivalent to 75 per cent of the legal minimum wage were given to: young workers under apprenticeship and occupational training contracts; and the long term unemployed aged over 25 (or below if they had family dependents) attending occupational training courses. The low-skilled unemployed aged under 25 following skill enhancing courses, and vocational or university students following on-the-job training received grants of Ptas 550-800 per day. Many of these programmes also benefited from social security contribution deductions.

49.   This figure should not be seen as a precise forecast but as an approximate indicator, since labour force growth is also subject to the uncertainties regarding general economic developments which will influence the participation rate.

50.   In addition the lower limit of 100 per cent of the legal minimum wage (LMW) for unemployment insurance benefits was reduced to 75 per cent of the LMW for unemployed workers without children.

51.   The withholding income tax on unemployment income above Ptas 1.1 million is 1 per cent, rising to 11 per cent for income over Ptas 1.8 million.

52.   The number of workers on job-training and vocational training schemes fell from about 500 000 on average in 1988-91 to some 100 000 in 1993. This marked fall also contributed to the rise in unemployment from mid-1992.

53.   Employers' social security contributions were halved if they hired the following for permanent jobs: *i)* unemployed persons under 26 years old; *ii)* the long-term unemployed over 45 years old; and *iii)* handicapped workers. Now only handicapped workers still benefit from this scheme.

54.   Weak control and the follow up of businesses opened under this scheme largely favoured fraud. Funds absorbed by this programme rose from Ptas 11 billion in 1985 to 111 billion in 1991.

55.   In August 1992 a law was passed shifting workers' sick leave pay from the 4th to the 15th day inclusive from the social security system to the firm (which already paid the first three days). This change seems to have reduced fraud. The budgetary savings on a full year basis is officially estimated to be 25 per cent of public spending on sick leave and temporary disability.

56.   Up to now the maximum ordinary working day is 9 hours and the maximum ordinary week 40 hours, so that more than 9 hours worked in a single day and more than 40 in a single week are counted as overtime work. Moreover, extraordinary and overtime hours worked could under the draft law be compensated with extra holidays.

57.   In the draft law changes affecting a small number of workers (*i.e.* up to 10 in firms with fewer than 100 workers, 10 per cent in firms with 100 to 300 workers, and up to 30 for firms with more than 300 workers) are treated as if they were "individual" cases.

58. The draft law gives the possibility (without employees' prior consent and administrative authorization) to employers to change working conditions, including dismissals, every 90 days.

59. The draft law excludes registered unemployed over 45 years, who could still be hired with a fixed-term contract under the employment promotion schemes. Moreover, the fundamental law, *Estatuto de los Trabajadores*, allows the Government to re-introduce by decree fixed-term contracts for all age groups for employment promotion purposes.

60. Fifteen per cent of work-time should be spent on theoretical training, but this time can be freely allocated at any time during the contract life. This type of contract will not entitle workers to unemployment or temporary invalidity payments. After an apprenticeship has been renewed for up to three years, a worker will no longer be eligible for another one in the same or a different firm.

61. After having a contract of this type renewed for a maximum of three years time, the worker is no longer eligible for another training contract by the same or different firm, in the same professional field.

62. An agreement was reached in December 1992 between employers, unions and the government that management of training of employed workers will be transferred to the social partners starting 1993. Employers contribute 0.6 per cent of salaries to social security for the funding of training programmes. Employers and unions will receive part of that contribution for their management of the programmes (0.1 per cent in 1993 to 0.3 per cent in 1996, half the total contribution, and will remain at that level thereafter).

63. At the same time limits were set for eligibility for unemployment and temporary sick leave payments and pension rights. Employees working less than 12 hours per week or 48 hours per month are not entitled to those benefits and, accordingly, do not pay social contributions for unemployment, temporary sick leave and pensions.

64. The draft law on the labour market reform has passed the lower house (*Congreso de los Diputados*) and is now in the Senate (*Senado*).

Bibliography

ALBA-RAMIREZ, A. and FREEMAN, R. B. (1990), "Job finding and wages when unemployment is really long: the case of Spain", *National Bureau of Economic Research Working Paper*, No. 3409, August.

ALBA-RAMIREZ, A. (1991), "Fixed-term employment contracts in Spain: Labour market flexibility or segmentation?", *Working Paper Universidad Carlos III de Madrid*, No. 91-29.

ANDRÉS, J. (1993), "La persistencia del desempleo agregado: una panorámica", *Moneda y Crédito*, No. 197.

BANCO DE ESPAÑA (1992), *Central de balances, resultados de las empresas no financieras*, Madrid.

BENTOLILA, S. and BLANCHARD, O.J. (1990), "Spanish Unemployment", *Economic Policy*, No. 10.

BLANCHARD, O. and SUMMERS, L. (1987), "Hysteresis and the European Unemployment Problem", *European Economic Review*, No. 31.

CALMFORS, L. (1993), "Centralisation of wage bargaining and macroeconomic performance – a survey", *OECD Economic Studies*, No. 21.

COE, D. T. (1985), "Nominal wages, the NAIRU and wage flexibility", *OECD Economic Studies*, No. 5.

COLEGIO DE ECONOMISTAS DE MADRID (1993), *Reforma del mercado de trabajo, Economistas,* No. 57, Madrid.

COMMISSION OF THE EUROPEAN COMMUNITIES (1993), "Growth, competitiveness, employment. The Challenges and ways forward into the 21st century", *White paper, COM(93)700*, Brussels.

DOLADO, J.J. and BENTOLILA, S. (1992), "Who are the insiders? Wage setting in Spanish manufacturing firms", *Documento de Trabajo Banco de España*, No. 9229, Madrid.

ELMESKOV, J. (1993), *High and persistent unemployment: assessment of the problem and its causes*, OECD, Economics Department Working Papers, No. 132, Paris.

ELMESKOV, J. and PICHELMANN, K. (1993), *Unemployment and labour force participation – trends and cycles*, OECD, Economics Department Working Papers, No. 130, Paris.

GARCÍA PEREA, P. and GÓMEZ, P. (1993), "Aspectos institucionales del mercado de trabajo español, en comparación con otros países comunitarios", *Boletín Económico*, Banco de España, September.

GIL, L. A. and JIMENO, J. F. (1993), "The determinants of labour mobility in Spain: who are the migrants?", *Documento de Trabajo Fundación de Estudios de Economía Aplicada*, No. 93-05, Madrid.

JIMENO, J. F. and TOHARIA, L. (1992), "Productivity and wage effects of fixed-term employment: evidence from Spain", *Documento de Trabajo Fundación de Estudios de Economía Aplicada*, No. 92-11, Madrid.

KAWASAKI, K. *et al.* (1990), *Modelling wages and prices for the smaller OECD countries*, OECD, Department of Economics and Statistics Working Papers, No. 86, Paris.

KLAU, F. and MITTELSTADT, A. (1986), "Labour market flexibility", *OECD Economic Studies*, No. 6.

LORENTE, J. R. (1992), "La dispersión geográfica de los salarios", *Síntesis Mensual de Indicadores Económicos*, Dirección General de Previsión y Coyuntura, Ministerio de Economía y Hacienda, September.

LORENTE, J. R. (1993), "Segmentación del mercado de trabajo y reformas estructurales", *Economistas, España 1993. Un balance*, Madrid.

MINISTERIO DE TRABAJO Y SEGURIDAD SOCIAL (1987), *Mercado de Trabajo en España durante 1987. Coyuntura y programas de actuación*, Colección Informes, Serie Empleo, Madrid.

MINISTERIO DE TRABAJO Y SEGURIDAD SOCIAL (1988), *La política de empleo en España*, Colección Informes, Serie Empleo. Madrid.

MINISTERIO DE TRABAJO Y SEGURIDAD SOCIAL (1991), *Estudios de economía del trabajo en España. III: El problema del paro*, Bentolila, S. and Toharia, L., Eds., Madrid.

OECD (1986), *Economic Surveys 1985/1986 – Spain*, Paris.

OECD (1991), "Unemployment benefit rules and labour market policy", *Employment Outlook*, Paris.

OECD (1992), "The public employment service in Japan, Norway, Spain and The United Kingdom", *Employment Outlook*, Paris.

OECD (1993), "Active labour market policies: assessing macroeconomic and microeconomic effects", *Employment Outlook*, Paris.

OECD (1993), *The tax/benefit position of production workers*, Paris.

OLIVEIRA, J. (1993), *Market structure, international trade and relative wages*, OECD, Economics Department Working Papers, No. 134.

Annex I

Labour market reforms of the 1980s

Active labour market policies started to be introduced in the early 1980s. A comprehensive package was passed by Parliament in 1984 modifying earlier laws and introducing new measures, with and without economic incentives, to promote employment creation. The most significant employment promotion programmes of the 1980s were the following:

Without economic incentives

Fixed-term (temporary) contracts not related to specific duration projects were introduced as a general employment promotion measure; restrictions on part-time employment were lifted; workers up to three years before the legal retirement age were allowed to retire on a part-time basis and be replaced by unemployed workers hired for part-time work; firms starting a new activity were allowed to hire people on fixed-term contracts.[1]

With economic incentives

A few programmes provided financial incentives for indefinite duration (permanent) employment contracts to specific small groups (*e.g.* handicapped persons, long-term unemployed aged over 45 years, women with difficulties in finding jobs, etc.) and for the transformation of temporary into permanent contracts. But the most important programmes (on-the-job training contracts and vocational training contracts) were designed to promote temporary employment, mainly of young people, the age category with by far the highest unemployment rate. These two programmes accounted for the majority of people hired under the employment promotion programmes with economic incentives, before the subsidies and grants were withdrawn in 1992 (see Table A1). Vocational training contracts (*contratos para la formación*) applied to non-qualified workers aged 16-20 and required theoretical training during ¼ to ½ of the work day. Employers offering these contracts could benefit from a reduction in their social security contributions amounting to 90-100 per cent and after 1988 a subsidy of Ptas 90 per hour of theoretical training was given either to the firm or to the educational centre providing the courses. On-the-job training contracts (*contratos en prácticas*) applied to unemployed with at least a secondary school or vocational diploma obtained in the preceding four years. For a full-time contract, employers obtained a 75 per cent reduction in their social security contributions and, if the unemployed had been on the unemployment register for at least two years, the employer obtained an additional grant of Ptas 280 000. Another major employment promotion programme is the temporary hiring of unemployed workers by different public administrations for public works or other activities of a social interest. These jobs could be subsidised by INEM (the National Employment Agency) to the tune of 40-75 per cent of the wage bill and up to 100 per cent for contracts given by local authorities. These programmes take the form of joint ventures (*convenios*) between the public administration and INEM, and entitlement to subsidies requires that at least 75 per cent of hired workers should have been registered as unemployed (50 per cent in case of contracting out the project). The maximum duration of all temporary employment contracts (without or with economic incentives) was set at 3 years (the same limit applied in the case of renewals of contracts of shorter duration).

In addition to these active labour market policies, a scheme with active and passive labour market policy elements applying to temporary (seasonal) farm workers in Andalucía and Extremadura, the two poorest regions, was also introduced in 1984, replacing a more limited scheme introduced a few years before. Under the active component, known as PER (Rural Employment Programme), rural unemployed people registered as unemployed are hired to work in projects co-financed by the State, Regions and INEM. Contracts offered to workers for these projects are subject to particularly flexible conditions regarding minimum duration. With at least 60 days of work per year (or at least 7 days per month) during which workers pay their social security contributions, they are entitled to receive a special unemployment benefit (TEAS) during the rest of the year (the month). This passive labour policy element has over the years taken the form of an income-support measure, attracting a considerable number of women to register as unemployed and receive the unemployment benefit. As a result, from less than 10 per cent in 1984, women accounted for 55 per cent of total recipients of the TAES in 1993. Some 200 000 people were covered by this scheme in 1992 and 1993 (the record was 295 000 in 1989-90), which is 1.3 per cent of the labour force. Because of the work they produce, the people under this scheme are not counted as registered unemployed.

Note

1. Fixed-term contracts for specific duration projects already existed, and the 1984 legislation made possible the hiring of workers with fixed-term contracts not necessarily assigned to specific duration projects. The latter was considered to be a temporary measure aimed at moderating the rapid growth of unemployment, as experienced after 1980. The other measures were considered to be permanent.

Table A1. **Hiring under employment promotion programmes**

Thousands

	1984	1985	1987	1990	1991	1992	1993[1]
Without economic incentives	**283.5**	**557.0**	**889.1**	**1 589.1**	**1 617.4**	**1 399.7**	**1 183.6**
Fixed-term contracts	235.4	432.2	666.6	1 174.9	1 142.8	856.5	544.8
Part-time contracts	47.7	121.9	220.8	410.9	470.9	539.7	635.9
Part-time workers hired to replace partially retired workers	0.3	1.9	0.9	2.3	2.6	2.2	1.6
Replacement of workers retired at age 64 (fixed-term contracts)	0.1	1.0	0.8	1.0	1.1	1.3	1.3
With economic incentives	**148.9**	**499.1**	**771.8**	**728.2**	**639.8**	**419.7**	**327.7**
Fixed-term contracts	142.0	434.7	639.3	715.4	628.4	385.4	283.8
Vocational training[2]	27.4	112.7	218.2	303.9	262.8	137.7	55.1
On-the-job training[2]	14.0	51.8	128.2	212.9	187.1	109.3	55.6
Public administration-INEM agreements	100.6	270.2	292.9	198.6	178.5	138.4	173.1
Indefinite contracts	6.9	64.4	132.5	12.8	11.4	34.3	43.9
Young workers	. .	55.8	118.5	. .	. .	1.9	1.9
Handicapped workers	1.7	2.2	3.5	3.9	4.0	4.5	5.8
Part-time workers hired to replace retired workers[3]	. .	. .	. .	. .	. .	0.2	0.1
Women[3]	. .	. .	. .	. .	. .	0.5	0.5
Workers aged over 45	5.2	6.4	10.5	8.9	7.4	6.4	4.7
Conversion of fixed-term into indefinite contracts[3]	. .	. .	. .	. .	. .	20.8	30.9
Total	**432.4**	**1 056.1**	**1 660.9**	**2 317.3**	**2 257.2**	**1 819.4**	**1 511.3**

1. Provisional data.
2. Economic incentives were discontinued in April 1992.
3. Measures introduced in 1992.
Source: Ministry of Labour and Social Affairs, *Boletín de Estadísticas Laborales.*

Table A2.   **Temporary workers as a percentage of total dependent employment, 1983-91**

	1983	1985	1987	1988	1989	1990	1991
Australia	..	..	21.2	18.7	19.9	19.3	19.7
Belgium	5.4	5.7	5.1	5.0	5.1	5.3	5.1
Denmark	..	12.3	11.1	11.5	10.0	10.8	11.9
Finland	11.1	10.7	11.2	..	11.9	..	13.1
France	3.3	4.7	7.1	7.8	8.5	10.5	10.2
West Germany	..	10.0	11.6	11.4	11.0	10.5	9.5
Greece	16.3	21.2	16.6	17.6	17.2	16.6	14.7
Ireland	6.2	7.3	8.6	9.1	8.6	8.5	8.3
Italy	6.6	4.8	5.4	5.8	6.3	5.2	5.4
Japan	10.3	10.4	10.5	10.7	10.8	10.7	10.5
Luxembourg	3.2	4.7	3.5	3.7	3.4	3.4	3.3
Netherlands	5.8	7.6	9.4	8.7	8.5	7.6	7.7
Portugal	..	..	16.9	18.5	18.7	18.6	16.5
Spain	..	..	**15.6**	**22.4**	**26.6**	**29.8**	**32.2**
Turkey	..	..	..	7.2	6.9	5.2	6.6
United Kingdom	5.5	7.0	6.3	6.0	5.4	5.2	5.3

Source: OECD (July 1993), ''Labour market prospects and recent developments'', *Employment Outlook.*

Diagram A1.   **PUBLIC SPENDING ON LABOUR MARKET POLICIES**
Per cent of GDP

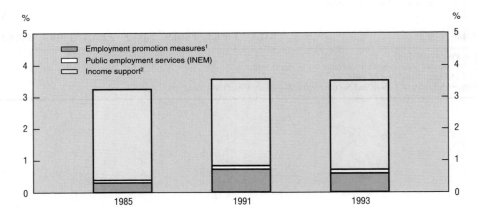

1. In this diagram subsidies and grants to people participating in training schemes are included in the employment promotion measures.
2. Mainly unemployment benefits.
Source: OECD.

Diagram A2. **RECIPIENTS OF INCOME SUPPORT**

Per cent of the labour force

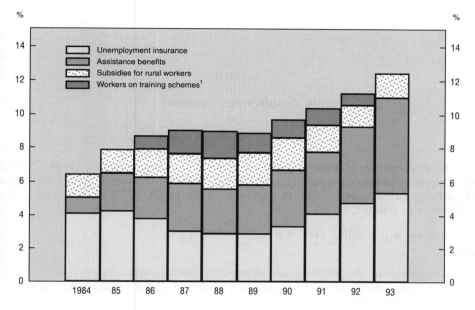

1. Data refers to participants in training programmes covering young unemployed, long-term unemployed and rural workers, who receive associated grants or wage subsidies in addition to subsidised training costs. No data is available for the years 1984, 1985 and 1993.
Source: Data submitted by national authorities.

Annex II

A simple wage equation

To examine the relationship between wages and unemployment a simple Phillips curve equation has been estimated on annual data 1973-93. The specification follows that of previous OECD studies[1] and, in particular of the OECD INTERLINK model. The equation is as follows:

$$w = a + b_*p + c_*lu + D_*X + e$$

where

    w = growth in compensation per employee in the business sector
    p = expected inflation, defined as a two period moving average of the private consumption deflator
    lu = natural logarithm of the unemployment rate
    X = vector of other relevant variables, such as productivity growth and a proxy for the tax wedge[2]
    e = error term

The equation is estimated by Ordinary Least Squares (OLS) and results are reported in Table A3. The statistical properties of the regression are good. Inflation expectations are backward looking, a reasonable assumption given the high degree of wage indexation and supported by the regression results. No money illusion is found, price changes are fully passed through to wages within the year. As in previous estimations for Spain, a non-linear specification (natural logs) of the unemployment variable gives the best fit. As a consequence the elasticity of wages with respect to the unemployment rate depends on the initial level of unemployment. Table A4 presents nominal wage elasticities for different unemployment rates. The rising unemployment rate since the beginning of the 1980s has been accompanied by increasingly low wage responsiveness.

Trend productivity, defined as a two year moving average of measured labour productivity in the non-farm business sector, makes a significant contribution to explaining growth in labour compensation. Results show that 66 per cent of the gains in underlying productivity are translated into wage increases. The tax wedge proxy, although significantly contributing to explaining the dependent variable, shows an estimated coefficient smaller than expected (should be close to one) reflecting errors in the measure of this variable due to constraints on data availability.

Notes and references

1. See, for instance, Kawasaki *et al.* (1990) and Coe (1985).
2. An approximate measure of the tax wedge is obtained from national accounts figures as follows: the sum of total household income taxes and total social security contributions is divided by total employment (thus assuming a same share for all employed) and that is divided by the private compensation per employee.

Table A3. **Wage equation estimation results (OLS)**[1]

Explanatory variable	Estimated coefficients	T-statistic
Inflation[2]	0.996	9.97
Unemployment rate[3]	-6.277	-6.85
Productivity growth[4]	0.663	2.853
Tax-wedge[5]	0.286	2.751
Constant	7.930	2.694

1. Ordinary least squares regression. Estimation period 1973-93. Where: R2 = 0.97, D.W. = 2.00 and S.E.E. = 1.42.
2. Inflation is defined as a two year moving average of current and past change in the private consumption deflator.
3. The unemployment rate is specified in natural logs.
4. A two-period moving average of productivity growth in the non-farm business sector is used.
5. A tax-wedge proxy is computed as total contributions (personal income taxes plus social security) per person employed divided by private compensation per employee.
Source: OECD.

Table A4. **Nominal wage elasticity with respect to unemployment rate**

Unemployment rate	Elasticity
5	-1.3
10	-0.63
15	-0.42
20	-0.31

Source: OECD.

Table A5. **Employment responsiveness to output**[1]

Business sector, growth rates

	Constant	b-parameter	R2	D.W.	S.E.E.
Spain[2]	**−3.20** (−8.0)	**1.06** (8.3)	**0.78**	**1.9**	**1.22**
France	−1.24 (−5.6)	0.43 (6.3)	0.65	1.5	0.61
West Germany	−1.02 (−2.9)	0.50 (4.7)	0.51	0.9	1.19
Italy	−0.37 (−1.5)	0.28 (4.2)	0.46	1.4	0.77
Japan	0.10 (0.4)	0.26 (4.1)	0.46	1.3	0.59
United Kingdom	−1.20 (−2.7)	0.52 (3.9)	0.42	1.3	1.67
United States	0.16 (0.4)	0.65 (6.0)	0.63	1.5	1.30

1. Ordinary least squares regression of the form $E = a + bQ + error$, where E is employment growth and Q is output growth; t-statistics are presented in parentheses.
2. The years 1972 and 1973 for Spain and 1972 for Japan are treated as outlyers and have been taken out of the regression analysis.
Source: OECD estimates.

Table A6. **Tax wedge proxy**[1]

	Per cent		1992 relative to 1970	Annual percentage change	
	1970	1992	(1970 = 1)	1970-92	1990-92
Spain	**13**	**40**	**3.1**	**9.8**	**4.0**
France	31	47	1.5	3.5	2.2
Netherlands	34	43	1.3	8.0	1.2
Italy	25	47	1.9	5.4	1.1
United Kingdom	25	26	1.0	0.3	0.0
Canada	21	32	1.5	3.6	0.0
United States	26	32	1.2	1.8	−1.5
Japan	13	25	1.9	5.6	0.0

1. Total direct taxes plus social security contributions per person employed as a per cent of private compensation per employee.
Source: OECD estimates.

Diagram A3. EMPLOYMENT RESPONSIVENESS TO OUTPUT IN THE BUSINESS SECTOR

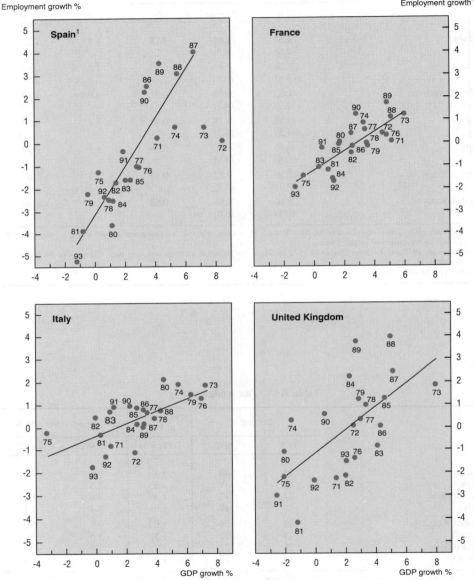

1. The points corresponding to 1972 and 1973 have been excluded from the regression calculation.
Source: OECD.

110

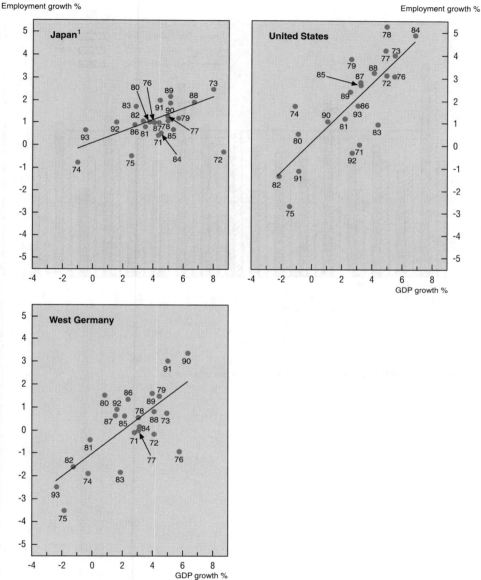

Diagram A3. *(cont'd)* EMPLOYMENT RESPONSIVENESS TO OUTPUT IN THE BUSINESS SECTOR

1. The point corresponding to 1972 has been excluded from the regression calculation.
Source: OECD.

Diagram A4. **REGIONAL UNEMPLOYMENT RATES**
Per cent of total labour force

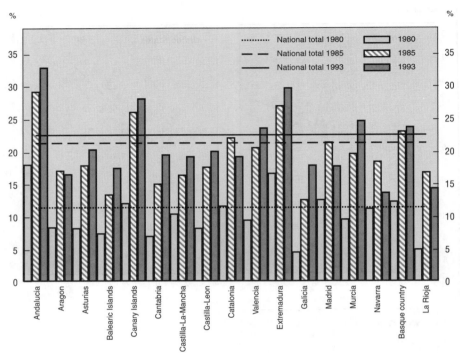

Source: National Institute of Statistics and Ministry of Economy and Finance.

Calendar of main economic events

1993

January

New VAT rates are applicable, the highest VAT rate of 28 per cent is replaced by the normal 15 per cent rate, a new car registration tax of 13 per cent is introduced to compensate for the loss of tax revenue and a new super-reduced VAT rate of 3 per cent is introduced for some basic products.

Some administered prices are revised: post office rates rise by 6.1 per cent, electricity fees rise 2.9 per cent on average and gasoline prices fall 50 cents per litre.

The Bank of Spain cuts its intervention rate from 13.75 per cent to 13.25 per cent.

The interest rate on twelve-month Treasury bills is lowered by 0.70 of a point to 13.04 per cent.

The Treasury lowers long-term interest rates: by 0.78 of a point on three year bonds to 12.52 per cent, by 0.70 of a point on five year bonds to 12.26 per cent, and by 0.56 of a point on ten year bonds to 11.96 per cent.

February

The Government approved a Ptas 62 000 package to help reactivate the economy. The main measures are: new credits for public infrastructure which together with EC cohesion funds amount to Ptas 300 billion for the years 1993 and 1994; special amortisation coefficients for new investment projects; the provision of special credit lines to medium and small-size enterprises; and the one year extension of fixed term contracts reaching the maximum three year extension limit during 1993.

The Bank of Spain cuts its intervention rate by 0.25 of a point to 13 per cent.

The interest rate on twelve-month Treasury bills is lowered by 0.50 of a point to 12.54 per cent.

Interest rates on three-month Treasury bills are lowered by 0.71 of a point to 12.85 per cent and on six-month Treasury bills by 0.69 of a point to 12.74 per cent.

April

The Treasury lowers long-term interest rates: by 0.52 of a point to 12 per cent on three year bonds, by 0.48 of a point to 11.78 per cent on five year bonds, and by 0.43 of a point to 11.53 per cent on ten year bonds.

May

The peseta is devalued by 8 per cent to a new ECU central parity of Ptas 154.25 per ECU. This is accompanied by a cut in the Bank of Spain's intervention rate to 11.50 per cent from 13 per cent and by an additional 0.25 of a point to 11.25 per cent shortly after.

The interest rate on the twelve-month Treasury bills is lowered by 1.5 percentage points to 11 per cent.

The interest rates on three-month and six-month Treasury bills are lowered by 1.88 and 1.93 percentage points from 12.85 and 12.73 per cent respectively.

June

The interest rate on twelve-month Treasury bills is lowered from 10.98 per cent to 10.08 per cent.

The Treasury lowers long-term interest rates on: three-year Treasury bonds by 1.36 percentage points to 10.64 per cent, five-year bonds by 1.12 percentage points to 10.66 per cent, and ten-year bonds by 0.48 of a point to 11.05 per cent.

General elections are held the 6th. The Socialist Party, though losing the absolute majority in Parliament, forms the new government.

The Second Directive on EC Banking Co-ordination, liberalising banking services, is incorporated in a Decree since the Parliament's discussion of the draft banking law was discontinued by the call for General elections.

July

The Bank of Spain cuts its intervention rate by 0.25 percentage points to 11 per cent.

The Bank of Spain lifts all restrictions on buying and selling of domestic currency bills.

The Treasury lowers long-term interest rates: by 0.76 of a point to 9.88 per cent on three year bonds, by 0.69 of a point to 9.97 per cent on five year bonds, and by 0.86 of a point to 10.19 per cent on ten year bonds.

August

The Bank of Spain cuts its intervention rate by 0.50 of a point to 10.50 per cent.

Strong pressures on several EMS currencies lead EC Economic ministers and Central Bank governors to widen the EMS fluctuation bands from 6 to 15 per cent.

The interest rate on twelve-month Treasury bills is lowered twice by 0.24 and 0.18 of a point to 9.66 per cent.

September

The Treasury lowers long-term interest rates: by 1.22 percentage points to 8.66 per cent on the three-year bonds, by 1.21 percentage points to 8.76 per cent on the five-year bonds, and by 1.18 percentage points to 9.01 percent on the ten-year bonds.

The Bank of Spain cuts its intervention rate by 0.50 of a point to 10 per cent.

The interest rate on twelve-month Treasury bills is lowered by 0.48 of a point to 9.18 per cent.

The Bank of Spain lowers the compulsory reserve ratio from 3 per cent to 2 per cent.

October

The interest rate on twelve-month Treasury bills is lowered by 0.35 of a point to 8.83 per cent.

The Bank of Spain lowers its intervention rate twice, by 0.50 and 0.25 of a point, respectively, to a cumulative 9.25 per cent.

The Treasury cuts interest rates in long-term bonds: by 0.59 of a point to 8.07 per cent on the three-year bonds, by 0.62 of a point to 8.14 per cent on the five-year bonds, and by 0.49 of a point to 8.52 per cent on the ten-year bonds.

An agreement is reached to reform the financing of the regions. Starting in 1994, 15 per cent of the region's revenues in personal income taxes will be included in the region's participation in State receipts. For the regions of Aragón, Madrid and Baleares the agreement will be delayed until the transfer of competences is finished and the regions opposed to the agreement, Galicia, Extremadura and Castilla-Leon, will be given the option to continue with the old financing system. Upper and lower limits are set to the growth of financial transfers to prevent this measure from excessively rising budgetary costs.

November

The interest rate on twelve-month Treasury bills is lowered by 0.29 of a point to 8.54 per cent.

December

The Government approves the measures for the reform of the labour market. They are contained in:
- a draft law modifying the current law regulating employment. It introduces flexibility in working schedules, facilitates functional and geographical mobility as well as dismissals of permanent workers, eliminates temporary contracts for the purpose of employment promotion, and introduces some flexibility in wage negotiations;
- a decree which introduces an apprenticeship contract, modifies training contracts, lifts all remaining restrictions on part-time contracts, authorises the extension for one more year of fixed-term contracts reaching the maximum three year duration during 1994, and legalises private placement agencies and short-term employment enterprises;
- a draft law regulating short-term employment enterprises.

The minimum legal wage and pensions for 1994 are raised by 3.5 per cent and the latter will be revised if actual inflation exceeds 3.5 per cent.

The Bank of Spain cuts its intervention rate by 0.25 of a point to 9 per cent.

The interest rate in twelve-month Treasury bills falls in three steps by 0.74 of a point to 7.80 per cent.

The Parliament approves the 1994 Budget.

The Government approves a decree regulating minimum shopping hours and allowing regional governments to fix shopping hours for their regions above that minimum. Shops will open a minimum of 72 hours per week Monday to Saturday and eight Sundays and holidays.

Because of the fragile financial situation of Banesto, one of the large commercial banks, the Bank of Spain intervenes and changes its management to safeguard its viability.

1994

January

The September agreement of a 3 per cent reduction in prices of pharmaceutical products covered by the social security becomes effective.

The Bank of Spain cuts its intervention rate by 0.25 of a point to 8.75 per cent.

Administered prices are raised: electricity prices by 2.06 per cent, cigarettes by 16.8 per cent, alcohol by 4.5 per cent, and mailing services by 3.47 per cent.

February

The Bank of Spain cuts its intervention rate by 0.25 of a point to 8.5 per cent.

March

The Bank of Spain lowers its intervention rate by 0.5 percentage points to 8 per cent.

April

The Bank of Spain lowers its intervention rate by 0.25 percentage points to 7.75 per cent.

STATISTICAL ANNEX

Table A. Main aggregates of national accounts
Billion pesetas

	Current prices					1986 prices				
	1988	1989	1990	1991	1992[1]	1988	1989	1990	1991	1992[1]
I. Expenditure										
1. Private consumption	25 179.6	28 366.9	31 278.8	34 213.0	37 175.7	22 683.7	23 965.9	24 820.4	25 543.5	26 076.5
2. Government consumption	5 924.4	6 831.3	7 756.0	8 808.4	9 900.7	5 368.1	5 813.5	6 140.8	6 474.2	6 717.5
3. Gross fixed capital formation	9 083.1	10 867.6	12 316.3	13 126.2	12 920.2	8 178.5	9 289.8	9 947.8	10 116.9	9 720.8
4. Changes in stocks	419.3	448.5	464.3	401.0	531.7	385.3	393.7	398.2	336.3	435.8
5. Exports of goods and services	7 574.8	8 150.4	8 555.1	9 409.4	10 357.9	7 169.2	7 384.0	7 621.5	8 221.1	8 773.2
6. *less*: Imports of goods and services	8 022.5	9 620.5	10 250.7	11 137.3	12 034.2	7 874.9	9 235.5	9 955.3	10 852.3	11 566.2
7. Gross Domestic Product at market prices	40 158.7	45 044.1	50 119.9	54 820.6	58 852.0	35 910.0	37 611.4	38 973.4	39 839.7	40 157.5
II. Value added by sector										
1. Agriculture, forestry and fishing	2 128.6	2 179.6	2 329.9	2 231.9	2 072.5	2 091.7	1 953.5	2 016.6	1 978.6	1 936.3
2. Industry	11 062.1	12 148.5	12 850.9	13 439.9	13 666.7	10 322.1	10 698.6	10 870.5	10 898.2	10 781.4
3. Construction	3 021.8	3 764.2	4 567.9	5 106.8	5 056.7	2 508.7	2 848.1	3 136.6	3 251.4	3 109.1
4. Services	21 321.1	23 946.2	27 229.4	30 640.0	34 195.0	18 828.2	19 803.5	20 601.9	21 288.3	21 889.3
5. Net indirect taxes	2 625.0	3 005.6	3 141.8	3 402.0	3 861.2	2 159.2	2 307.8	2 347.8	2 423.3	2 441.4
III. National income										
1. Compensation of employees						18 235.8	20 478.0	23 241.6	25 572.6	27 253.0
2. Gross operating surplus						18 676.5	20 840.9	22 829.9	24 851.4	26 491.8
Households and private non profit institutions						10 719.8	11 795.2	13 171.8	14 507.8	..
Corporate and quasi-corporate enterprises						7 561.3	8 600.5	9 149.5	9 768.8	..
General government						395.4	445.2	508.5	574.9	..
3. *less*: Consumption of fixed capital						4 599.8	5 033.3	5 521.6	5 994.0	6 389.2
4. Net national income at factor cost						32 312.4	36 285.6	40 549.8	44 430.0	47 355.6

1. Provisional data.
Source: National Institute of Statistics, *Contabilidad Nacional* (1994) and Bank of Spain, *Cuentas financieras* (1993).

Table B. Income and outlay transactions of households

Billion pesetas

	1986	1987	1988	1989	1990	1991	1992[1]
1. Compensation of employees	14 626.1	16 347.7	18 235.8	20 478.0	23 241.6	25 572.6	27 253.0
2. Property and entrepreneurial income, gross	8 576.9	9 602.4	10 719.8	11 795.2	13 171.8	14 507.8	..
3. Other income from property	1 317.9	1 332.7	1 469.0	1 696.9	1 789.8	2 072.8	..
4. Current transfers	5 626.3	6 254.5	6 930.3	7 853.1	8 989.7	10 292.6	..
of which:							
Social security and social assistance benefits	4 767.7	5 289.5	5 860.3	6 617.4	7 733.3	8 971.3	10 317.0
5. Change in the actuarial reserves for pensions	168.1	154.6	396.5	262.5	252.8	309.3	..
6. **Current receipts**	30 315.2	33 691.9	37 751.3	42 085.7	47 445.7	52 755.0	..
7. Final consumption expenditure	20 437.7	22 855.8	25 179.6	28 366.9	31 278.8	34 213.0	37 175.7
8. Direct taxes on income and property	1 960.0	2 741.7	3 152.0	3 860.4	4 297.9	4 963.9	5 764.1
9. Current transfers	5 264.1	5 885.8	6 581.1	7 261.0	8 302.2	9 290.5	..
of which:							
Social security and social assistance contributions	3 908.8	4 420.5	4 820.6	5 525.9	6 318.7	7 018.9	..
10. **Current disbursements**	27 661.9	31 483.3	34 912.6	39 488.4	43 878.9	48 467.4	..
11. Disposable income (6-8-9)	23 091.1	25 064.4	28 018.3	30 964.2	34 845.6	38 500.6	41 126.4
12. Gross saving (11-7)	2 653.3	2 208.6	2 838.7	2 597.3	3 566.8	4 287.7	3 950.7
13. Saving rate, per cent (12/11)	11.5	8.8	10.1	8.4	10.2	11.1	9.6

1. Provisional data.
Source: National Institute of Statistics, *Contabilidad Nacional* (1994) and Bank of Spain, *Cuentas financieras* (1993).

Table C. **Public sector accounts**

Billion pesetas

	1988	1989	1990	1991	1992[1]
	1. General government				
Current account					
Receipts					
Gross operating surplus	395.4	445.2	508.5	574.9	..
Property income receivable	312.7	396.1	485.9	722.3	..
Indirect taxes	4 162.1	4 657.3	4 976.5	5 399.9	6 036.2
Direct taxes	4 196.6	5 430.6	6 017.9	6 604.8	7 288.6
Actual social contributions	4 676.9	5 396.7	6 110.1	6 784.1	8 235.5[2]
Imputed social contributions	351.1	364.3	426.8	471.9	..
Miscellaneous current transfers	871.4	912.6	985.0	1 187.5	..
Total	14 966.0	17 602.9	19 510.6	21 745.5	24 238.5
Disbursements					
Final consumption expenditure	5 924.4	6 831.3	7 756.0	8 808.4	9 900.7
Property income payable	1 345.9	1 560.5	1 775.5	2 172.8	2 490.0
Subsidies	829.6	888.9	960.7	991.7	983.4
Social security benefits	5 567.2	6 276.6	7 221.2	8 366.6	9 529.9
Miscellaneous current transfers	591.0	739.9	762.0	928.4	947.2
Gross saving	707.9	1 305.7	1 035.3	477.6	387.3
Capital account					
Receipts					
Gross saving	707.9	1 305.7	1 035.3	477.6	387.3
Capital transfers	126.3	203.3	206.9	319.8	314.8
Capital taxes	98.5	104.8	117.0	106.6	125.1
Total	932.7	1 613.8	1 359.2	904.1	827.2
Disbursements					
Gross fixed capital formation	1 476.3	1 975.2	2 492.3	2 722.5	2 598.4
Capital transfers	697.6	874.7	739.5	818.4	850.4
Net purchases of land and intangible assets	64.8	23.0	90.4	62.2	..
Net lending (+) or net borrowing (−)	−1 305.9	−1 259.2	−1 963.1	−2 699.1	−2 621.6
(per cent of GDP)	(−3.3)	(−2.8)	(−3.9)	(−4.9)	(−4.5)

1. Provisional data. Gross fixed capital formation includes net purchases of land and intangible assets.
2. Actual plus imputed social contributions.
Source: National Institute of Statistics, *Contabilidad Nacional* (1994) and Bank of Spain, *Cuentas financieras* (1993).

Table C. **Public sector accounts** *(cont'd)*
Billion pesetas

	1988	1989	1990	1991	1992
	2. Central government				
1. Tax revenue	6 834.2	8 340.4	8 823.4	9 632.3	..
2. Property and entrepreneurial income (gross)	222.0	281.6	326.1	557.0	..
3. Current transfers	1 214.5	1 336.3	1 422.5	1 597.7	..
4. **Total current revenue**	8 270.7	9 958.3	10 572.1	11 787.0	..
5. Purchase of goods and services	2 559.8	2 845.1	3 064.7	3 353.2	..
6. Current transfers	4 322.1	5 031.0	5 426.5	6 172.0	..
7. Subsidies	529.0	527.7	546.1	509.2	..
8. Other	1 155.8	1 328.7	1 479.4	1 759.2	..
9. **Total current expenditure**	8 566.6	9 732.6	10 516.7	11 793.5	..
10. Gross saving	−70.5	470.3	325.0	288.4	..
11. Capital taxes	21.3	17.3	1.4	0.9	..
12. Capital transfers	160.6	166.8	133.7	162.8	..
13. **Total capital resources**	111.4	654.4	460.2	452.1	..
14. Gross fixed capital formation	484.3	620.9	852.9	894.6	..
15. Net purchases of land and intangible assets	19.0	19.4	27.6	40.1	..
16. Capital transfers	781.2	999.0	933.6	896.1	..
17. **Total capital expenditure**	1 284.5	1 639.3	1 814.1	1 830.8	..
18. Overall financial surplus (+) or deficit (−)	−1 173.1	−984.9	−1 354.0	−1 378.7	..

Source: National Institute of Statistics, *Contabilidad Nacional* (1994) and Bank of Spain, *Cuentas financieras* (1993).

Table C. **Public sector accounts** *(cont'd)*

Billion pesetas

	1988	1989	1990	1991	1992
	3. Territorial government [1]				
1. Tax revenue	1 524.5	1 747.5	2 170.9	2 372.5	..
2. Property and entrepreneurial income (gross)	61.9	87.6	125.9	129.1	..
3. Current transfers	1 806.0	2 046.6	2 288.2	2 597.9	..
4. **Total current revenue**	3 392.3	3 881.7	4 584.9	5 099.5	..
5. Purchase of goods and services	2 010.2	2 324.9	2 784.6	3 236.6	..
6. Current transfers	391.7	503.6	588.7	739.2	..
7. Other	432.7	528.1	647.8	806.6	..
8. **Total current expenditure**	2 834.6	3 356.5	4 021.1	4 782.5	..
9. Gross saving	678.7	670.2	738.9	524.7	..
10. Capital taxes	77.2	87.5	115.6	105.7	..
11. Capital transfers	278.6	411.0	499.5	550.1	..
12. **Total capital resources**	1 034.5	1 168.7	1 354.0	1 180.5	..
13. Gross fixed capital formation	912.8	1 231.4	1 488.7	1 664.6	..
14. Net purchases of land and intangible assets	45.7	3.6	62.9	22.1	..
15. Capital transfers	204.2	297.6	311.8	391.0	..
16. **Total capital expenditure**	1 162.8	1 532.5	1 863.4	2 077.8	..
17. Overall financial surplus (+) or deficit (–)	–128.3	–363.8	–509.4	–897.3	..
	4. Social security institutions				
1. Social security contributions	4 629.4	5 338.2	6 048.3	6 715.1	..
2. Transfers	1 852.7	2 159.1	2 287.1	2 633.1	..
3. Other current receipts	67.3	56.4	109.4	161.9	..
4. **Total current receipts**	6 549.4	7 553.7	8 444.8	9 510.1	..
5. Purchase of goods and services	1 354.5	1 661.3	1 906.7	2 218.6	..
6. Social security benefits	4 989.9	5 632.1	6 492.7	7 527.4	..
7. Current subsidies and transfers	154.1	150.2	137.6	147.9	..
8. **Total current expenditure**	6 498.5	7 443.6	8 536.9	9 893.9	..
9. Gross saving	99.7	165.1	–28.7	–335.5	..
10. Gross fixed capital formation	79.2	123.0	150.7	163.2	..
11. Other	52.6	5.0	11.3	12.5	..
12. **Total capital expenditure**	131.7	128.0	162.0	175.7	..
13. Total income from capital	27.5	52.4	91.0	88.1	..
14. Overall financial surplus (+) or deficit (–)	–4.5	89.6	–99.7	–423.1	..

1. Regional and local government.
Source: National Institute of Statistics, *Contabilidad Nacional* (1994) and Bank of Spain, *Cuentas financieras* (1993).

Table D.   **Labour market**

	1986	1987	1988	1989	1990	1991	1992
	Thousands						
Civilian labour force [1]	14 071	14 407	14 633	14 819	15 020	15 073	15 155
Civilian employment [1]	11 111	11 452	11 781	12 258	12 579	12 609	12 366
Agriculture	1 784	1 728	1 694	1 598	1 486	1 345	1 253
Industry	2 697	2 764	2 804	2 898	2 978	2 890	2 804
Construction	849	932	1 021	1 134	1 220	1 274	1 196
Services	5 781	6 028	6 261	6 629	6 895	7 101	7 113
Employees, total	7 675	7 996	8 357	8 880	9 273	9 373	9 076
Unemployment	2 959	2 955	2 852	2 561	2 441	2 464	2 789
	Per cent						
Participation rate							
Total (all age groups)	48.9	49.4	49.6	49.5	49.7	49.5	49.2
Men	69.7	69.1	68.1	67.8	67.8	66.9	65.5
Women	30.0	31.5	32.5	32.8	33.4	33.6	34.2
Structure of the labour force according to education level							
Illiterate	2.0	1.9	1.8	1.7	1.5	1.4	1.4
Without studies	9.3	9.5	10.3	10.1	9.6	9.0	8.5
Primary degree	46.0	44.0	41.2	38.9	37.7	36.8	35.3
Secondary degree	36.4	39.2	41.7	43.8	45.6	46.8	48.7
University degree	4.5	4.7	4.9	5.4	5.6	5.9	6.1
Employment structure [2]							
Agriculture	16.1	15.1	14.4	13.0	11.8	10.7	10.1
Industry	24.3	24.1	23.8	23.6	23.7	22.9	22.7
Construction	7.6	8.1	8.7	9.3	9.7	10.1	9.7
Services	52.0	52.6	53.1	54.1	54.8	56.3	57.5
Unemployment [3]							
Total	21.0	20.5	19.5	17.3	16.3	16.3	18.4
Two years or more	9.1	11.1	10.9	9.7	8.6	8.3	8.3
Men	18.0	16.8	15.2	13.0	12.0	12.3	14.3
Women	27.4	28.0	27.7	25.4	24.2	23.8	25.6
Age 16 to 24	45.1	43.1	39.9	34.4	32.3	31.1	34.5
Age 25 to 54	15.3	15.0	14.7	13.7	13.1	13.7	15.7
Age 55 and over	8.9	8.9	8.4	8.2	7.6	8.0	9.0

1.   These exclude those who are on compulsory service but include the professional military as well as marginal workers.
2.   Per cent of total employment.
3.   Per cent of total labour force.
Source: Ministry of Economy and Finance, *Síntesis Mensual de Indicadores Económicos* (1994) and Ministry of Labour and Social Affairs, *Boletín de Estadísticas Laborales* (1993).

Table E. **Price and wage trends**

Percentage change at annual rate

	1986	1987	1988	1989	1990	1991	1992
				Prices			
Consumer prices	8.8	5.2	4.8	6.8	6.7	5.9	5.9
Food	10.6	5.0	3.7	7.7	6.5	3.5	3.7
Non-food	7.9	5.4	5.4	6.3	6.8	7.2	7.1
Energy	−6.3	−3.9	−0.6	2.6	8.2	7.6	6.7
Non-energy	9.9	5.8	5.1	7.0	6.6	5.8	5.9
Non-food and non-energy [1]	9.8	5.8	5.4	7.1	6.5	6.4	6.8
Industrial prices	0.9	0.8	2.9	4.2	2.2	1.5	1.4
Food	4.2	1.7	1.9	7.0	1.3	1.4	2.8
Non-food	5.6	4.8	3.3	3.2	3.6	4.7	3.2
Energy	−11.1	−7.0	0.5	2.9	5.5	3.3	2.3
Non-energy	3.1	1.8	3.3	4.3	1.8	1.2	1.3
Consumer goods	5.1	3.9	3.3	4.5	3.1	3.5	2.9
Investment goods	6.2	5.0	4.6	4.6	4.1	3.5	2.3
Intermediate goods	−3.1	−2.5	2.3	3.8	0.9	−0.7	−0.2
of which: Non-energy	0.2	−0.8	2.8	4.1	−0.4	−2.0	−1.0
Unit value of exports	−3.5	2.4	4.6	4.8	−2.5	−1.5	0.6
Unit value of imports	−17.4	−2.6	−1.4	2.3	−3.4	−2.9	−3.0
of which: Non-energy	−2.0	−0.1	1.5	0.9	−4.7	−2.8	−1.6
				Wages			
Average increase in contractual wages	8.2	6.5	6.4	7.8	8.3	8.0	7.3
Monthly earnings per employee	11.4	7.1	6.0	5.7	8.5	7.6	7.5
of which: Industry	12.0	7.7	5.8	4.7	8.5	8.8	8.0
Daily pay in agriculture	9.0	6.5	5.1	9.1	11.5	9.2	9.8
Salary cost per head in construction (including social security contributions)	9.4	7.3	7.0	9.9	13.0	11.1	6.0

1. Seasonal food and energy excluded.
Source: Ministry of Economy and Finance, *Síntesis Mensual de Indicadores Económicos* (1994), Ministry of Labour and Social Affairs, *Boletín de Estadísticas Laborales* (1993) and Bank of Spain, *Boletín Estadístico* (1994).

Table F. Money and credit
Billion pesetas

	1992			1993			
	Q2	Q3	Q4	Q1	Q2	Q3	Q4
	1. Monetary indicators *(quarterly changes)*						
M1	503.7	−333.9	42.4	−683.2	498.3	−280.7	1 014.8
Currency in circulation	158.3	91.5	320.4	−141.5	126.0	104.6	395.2
Sight deposits	345.4	−425.4	−278.1	−541.6	372.3	−385.2	619.5
Saving deposits	165.9	73.6	306.2	−381.0	184.5	149.5	774.1
Time deposits	357.6	630.3	644.5	1 092.8	825.4	654.8	218.5
M3	951.6	583.7	1 319.1	447.9	1 614.4	514.9	2 299.4
Other liquid assets in the hands of the public	−119.5	158.1	1 284.4	331.1	146.9	612.0	842.0
ALP (liquid assets in the hands of the public)	908.0	527.7	2 277.2	359.8	1 655.2	1 135.6	2 849.3

	1987	1988	1989	1990	1991	1992
	2. Monetary indicators *(end of period, levels)*					
A. ALP	34 794	39 444	45 278	50 686	56 439	59 375
a) M1	8 651	10 320	11 860	14 163	15 899	15 631
Currency in circulation	2 735	3 236	3 835	4 533	5 607	6 025
Sight deposits	5 916	7 083	8 025	9 630	10 292	9 607
b) M2	15 078	17 563	19 612	23 037	25 798	25 690
of which: Saving deposits	6 428	7 244	7 752	8 874	9 899	10 059
c) M3	31 724	35 778	40 897	46 309	51 301	53 700
of which: Time deposits	10 633	11 216	12 555	13 868	15 970	17 829
d) Other liquid assets in the hands of the public	9 083	10 664	13 112	13 781	14 671	15 856
B. Non-monetary liabilities	2 711	3 611	4 811	4 517	4 733	4 375
a) General government	1 420	1 768	2 804	2 700	2 888	2 992
b) Private sector	1 291	1 843	2 007	1 818	1 845	1 383
	3. Credit aggregates *(end of period, levels)*					
C. Internal credit	37 823	44 117	51 281	56 804	61 721	65 488
a) Credit to general government	12 170	13 698	16 147	18 175	18 530	19 597
Bank credits	2 417	2 367	2 863	3 561	4 729	5 353
Securities	10 655	10 774	11 336	12 485	10 716	10 506
Money market credits	1 133	863	1 493	2 025	3 211	4 116
Other	−2 035	−306	455	105	−125	−377
b) Credit to private sector	25 653	30 419	35 134	38 629	43 191	45 890
Bank credits	23 706	27 854	32 654	36 370	40 852	43 756
Securities	2 322	2 675	2 742	2 606	2 810	2 725
Money market credits	302	703	230	205	147	148
Other	−677	−812	−492	−552	−618	−739
D. Credit to foreign sector	2 745	3 034	2 913	2 541	3 747	3 960

Source: Bank of Spain, *Boletín Estadístico* (1994).

Table G. **Balance of payments**[1]
Million dollars

	1985	1986	1987	1988	1989	1990	1991	1992
Imports (fob)	27 740	33 164	46 234	57 573	67 777	83 175	89 444	94 858
Exports (fob)	23 550	26 714	33 399	39 570	43 221	53 679	58 635	64 012
Trade balance	-4 190	-6 449	-12 835	-18 003	-24 555	-29 496	-30 808	-30 846
Invisibles, net	5 834	9 245	10 150	9 805	9 013	8 396	8 111	6 614
of which:								
Tourism	7 083	10 443	12 779	14 233	13 173	14 215	14 604	16 593
Investment income	-1 806	-1 997	-2 753	-3 522	-2 970	-3 786	-4 827	-6 620
Transfers, net	1 099	1 126	2 615	4 508	4 607	4 236	5 992	5 885
Current balance	2 744	3 922	-70	-3 690	-10 935	-16 864	-16 705	-18 346
Private long-term capital	-1 274	489	9 301	10 324	16 451	17 225	32 639	16 861
Official long-term capital	-36	-2 131	-101	-875	503	1 673	1 030	4 803
Total long-term capital	-1 310	-1 642	9 200	9 449	16 954	18 898	33 669	21 664
Basic balance	1 434	2 281	9 130	5 758	6 019	2 033	16 964	3 318
Short-term capital[2]	107	134	1 855	456	-900	296	-2 903	-4 818
Errors and omissions	-1 875	63	-1 294	-2 355	-2 610	-4 263	-1 104	-5 365
Balance on non-monetary transactions	-334	2 478	9 692	3 860	2 509	-1 934	12 957	-6 864
Monetary movements								
(increase in assets = -)	1 878	219	-3 197	-4 387	-2 360	-8 700	-1 145	10 114
Changes in reserves (increase = -)	2 213	-2 261	-12 888	-8 247	-4 868	-6 766	-14 104	16 983

1. On a transactions basis.
2. Including bank's local accounts in foreign currency.
Source: OECD estimates.

Table H. Foreign trade[1]
1. By commodity
Billion pesetas

	1987	1988	1989	1990	1991	1992[2]
1. Imports, cif						
1. Live animals and related products	242.1	285.5	349.1	372.0	433.8	461.4
2. Vegetables	248.4	264.6	276.4	289.6	330.8	342.2
3. Oils and fats	23.9	25.4	34.8	28.9	43.2	44.8
4. Food products, beverages and tobacco	200.0	257.5	276.8	311.3	376.1	431.7
5. Mineral products	1 084.1	917.4	1 136.9	1 172.3	1 185.4	1 157.4
6. Chemicals and related products	539.9	599.1	672.1	704.8	779.2	861.2
7. Plastic materials	220.1	256.7	313.6	355.1	377.0	412.1
8. Leather, leather manufactures	98.2	103.8	107.8	94.6	101.9	104.3
9. Cork and wood products	77.1	100.0	129.9	130.3	123.6	130.5
10. Paper, articles of paper pulp	153.9	192.0	233.9	268.3	288.8	302.3
11. Textile and related products	216.0	259.3	342.6	403.4	513.9	600.2
12. Footwear, hat-making	17.7	23.9	24.5	31.9	47.2	56.3
13. Mineral manufactures, plaster, glass	68.9	80.0	97.5	107.3	120.4	124.5
14. Pearls, precious stones, jewellery	26.5	34.1	42.0	63.5	74.8	73.1
15. Manufactures of metal	402.6	517.6	626.0	642.4	663.0	669.3
16. Machinery and electrical machinery	1 329.5	1 779.8	2 091.4	2 208.2	2 351.9	2 341.7
17. Transport equipment	685.8	976.8	1 180.6	1 210.4	1 316.0	1 498.8
18. Optical instruments, photographic apparatus, sound equipment	307.5	258.4	308.5	359.0	350.4	359.4
19. Arms and ammunition	1.9	2.6	3.0	4.5	4.6	3.4
20. Furniture, toys, sporting goods	61.5	84.2	109.8	131.7	170.9	214.1
21. Works of art, antiques	24.1	20.7	39.2	25.2	19.4	16.2
Total	6 029.8	7 039.5	8 396.4	8 914.7	9 672.1	10 205.0
2. Exports, fob						
1. Live animals and related products	70.9	89.6	100.8	113.3	108.3	121.3
2. Vegetables	418.6	444.2	446.4	418.2	489.0	543.1
3. Oils and fats	64.1	79.6	48.0	92.5	118.4	60.4
4. Food products, beverages and tobacco	218.1	218.1	225.8	232.7	272.0	304.7
5. Mineral products	319.9	259.6	298.7	320.0	321.4	247.2

6. Chemicals and related products	298.0	325.7	327.5	343.1	360.7	390.7
7. Plastic materials	186.3	223.7	238.1	256.7	262.8	277.8
8. Leather, leather manufactures	88.1	78.6	79.1	72.7	64.6	72.2
9. Cork and wood products	44.0	43.5	48.2	51.8	50.1	55.1
10. Paper, articles of paper pulp	145.1	162.2	160.9	161.5	167.4	188.4
11. Textile and related products	196.2	210.7	208.9	228.5	240.1	253.6
12. Footwear, hat-making	140.6	134.8	134.9	157.0	141.8	135.4
13. Mineral manufactures, plaster, glass	114.5	139.2	157.0	171.3	185.1	216.9
14. Pearls, precious stones, jewellery	27.1	27.6	29.2	28.6	35.8	33.2
15. Manufactures of metal	419.7	474.6	532.6	539.7	572.7	565.6
16. Machinery and electrical machinery	564.8	640.9	760.0	868.1	978.3	1 070.8
17. Transport equipment	738.6	929.1	1 092.4	1 320.5	1 575.4	1 775.7
18. Optical instruments, photographic apparatus, sound equipment	37.9	39.5	45.5	53.1	62.4	78.5
19. Arms and ammunition	6.1	9.6	7.2	7.9	7.8	6.8
20. Furniture, toys, sporting goods	80.1	106.3	115.3	124.0	127.4	135.0
21. Works of art, antiques	16.9	49.3	78.1	81.9	83.9	73.4
Total	4 195.6	4 686.4	5 134.5	5 642.8	6 225.7	6 605.7

1. Customs clearance basis. New classification from 1988 onwards.
2. Provisional figures.
Source: Ministry of Economy and Finance.

2. By geographical area
Billion pesetas

	1987	1988	1989	1990	1991	1992[2]
	1. Imports, cif					
Total	6 029.8	7 039.5	8 396.4	8 914.7	9 672.1	10 205.0
OECD	4 457.9	5 453.7	6 520.8	7 014.1	7 615.0	8 064.9
of which: United States	499.1	626.6	762.7	744.8	770.5	755.0
Japan	270.2	361.1	401.6	395.2	451.5	475.6
Canada	26.4	30.6	41.2	44.4	46.2	58.3
EC	3 292.0	4 001.5	4 780.4	5 300.6	5 797.3	6 197.5
of which: United Kingdom	421.8	499.5	549.3	638.1	728.2	745.0
France	774.0	949.0	1 157.1	1 307.3	1 467.7	1 619.3
Germany	970.3	1 138.7	1 359.2	1 463.0	1 565.5	1 673.7
Italy	532.7	675.9	835.0	905.6	971.7	1 003.1
Portugal	100.7	146.3	196.6	222.8	263.3	275.8
Non OECD countries	1 571.9	1 585.8	1 875.6	1 900.6	2 057.2	2 140.1
Ex-COMECON	155.8	180.2	212.8	189.9	127.4	152.5
OPEC	572.6	471.0	625.3	640.6	694.8	600.8
Latin America[3]	362.6	365.2	388.3	384.3	405.4	418.7
Other	481.0	569.4	649.1	685.8	829.6	968.1
	2. Exports, fob					
Total	4 195.6	4 686.4	5 134.5	5 642.8	6 225.7	6 605.7
OECD	3 335.6	3 793.6	4 187.7	4 631.6	5 116.3	5 445.1
of which: United States	341.7	368.9	385.5	328.9	305.8	315.3
Japan	46.3	55.6	63.2	64.3	61.4	61.6
Canada	44.3	54.7	45.0	35.8	38.2	34.7
EC	2 676.7	3 074.8	3 432.8	3 910.4	4 417.0	4 701.1
of which: United Kingdom	398.0	458.9	516.6	507.2	477.9	505.7
France	786.9	865.1	1 000.6	1 173.1	1 244.4	1 335.0
Germany	503.4	562.0	616.3	756.0	992.6	1 036.5
Italy	371.9	453.7	484.9	603.8	706.7	719.4
Portugal	189.9	262.1	321.8	341.7	410.4	496.5
Non OECD countries	860.0	892.8	946.8	1 011.2	1 109.4	1 160.5
Ex-COMECON	66.9	59.8	79.2	66.8	85.2	84.8
OPEC	192.3	213.0	202.0	195.1	219.8	238.3
Latin America[3]	148.3	147.2	188.1	201.1	204.6	279.8
Other	452.5	472.8	477.6	548.1	599.8	557.6

1.   Customs clearance basis.
2.   Provisional data.
3.   Central and South America excluding Venezuela.
Source: Ministry of Economy and Finance.

Table I. **Foreign assets and liabilities**

Billion pesetas, end of period

	1988	1989	1990	1991	1992 [1]
Liabilities	12 498.4	15 289.2	19 680.9	24 536.1	30 149.2
Monetary institutions	5 058.6	5 960.9	8 149.1	9 189.2	11 436.1
Bank of Spain	92.7	87.6	50.7	46.7	52.4
Banking system	4 965.9	5 873.3	8 098.4	9 142.5	11 383.7
Government	692.2	959.8	1 298.6	3 082.0	3 579.2
Private sector	6 747.6	8 368.5	10 233.2	12 264.9	15 133.9
Assets	9 788.0	11 271.2	13 136.2	15 788.4	19 267.6
Monetary institutions	7 846.2	8 490.1	9 767.5	12 027.3	14 573.7
Bank of Spain	4 609.2	4 937.9	5 347.6	6 731.3	5 604.1
Banking system	3 237.0	3 552.2	4 419.9	5 296.0	8 969.6
Government	113.7	117.9	106.4	119.7	127.9
Private sector	1 828.1	2 663.2	3 262.3	3 641.4	4 566.0

1. Provisional data.
Source: Bank of Spain, *Cuentas financieras* (1993).

Table J. **Public sector**

	1980	1985	1990	1991	1992[1]
	Per cent of GDP				

A. Structure of government expenditure and tax receipts

	1980	1985	1990	1991	1992[1]
Expenditure, total	32.2	41.1	41.8	43.5	44.6
Current consumption	13.2	14.7	15.5	16.1	16.8
Transfers to households	13.9	16.0	15.9	17.0	17.8
Subsidies	1.9	2.4	1.9	1.8	1.7
Fixed investment	1.9	3.7	5.2	5.1	4.4
Other	1.2	4.3	3.3	3.5	3.9
Tax receipts, total	29.9	34.2	37.9	38.6	40.1
Income tax	7.0	8.5	12.0	12.0	12.4
of which:					
Personal income	5.3	6.5	8.6	9.1	9.8
Corporate profits	1.7	2.0	3.4	3.0	2.6
Social security contributions	13.1	13.0	13.0	13.2	14.0
Taxes on goods and services	6.6	9.5	9.9	9.9	10.3
Memorandum item:					
Net lending	-2.2	-6.9	-3.9	-4.9	-4.5

	1979[2]	1985	1990	1991	1992
	Per cent				

B. Taxation

	1979[2]	1985	1990	1991	1992
Personal income tax					
Lowest marginal rate	15.0	8.0	25.0	25.0	20.0
Highest marginal rate	65.0	66.0	56.0	56.0	56.0
Number of brackets	(28)	(34)	(16)	(16)	(17)
Marginal rate					
(for a single average production worker)	17.0	33.0	27.0	27.0	24.5
Average rate					
(for a single average production worker)	11.0	10.4	10.9	11.3	11.7
Social security contributions					
Marginal rate					
(for a single average production worker)	37.3	36.6	36.2	36.2	37.2
of which:					
Employees' contribution rate	5.5	6.0	6.0	6.0	6.0
Employers' contribution rate	31.8	30.6	30.2	30.2	31.2
VAT standard rate	n.a.	n.a.	12.0	12.0	15.0

1. Provisional data.
2. 1981 data for social security contributions.
Source: OECD, *National accounts* (1994) and *The tax/benefit position of production workers* (1993).

Table K.   **Production structure and performance indicators**

Per cent of total

	1981-87[1]	1988	1989	1990	1991	1992[2]
A. Production structure						
(factor cost, current prices)						
Agriculture	6.1	5.7	5.2	5.0	4.3	3.8
Industry	30.4	29.5	28.9	27.4	26.1	24.9
Construction	7.2	8.1	9.0	9.7	9.9	9.2
Services	56.2	56.8	57.0	58.0	59.6	62.2
B. Production structure						
(factor cost, 1986 prices)						
Agriculture	6.3	6.2	5.5	5.5	5.3	5.1
Industry	30.8	30.6	30.3	29.5	29.1	28.6
Construction	7.1	7.4	8.1	9.0	8.7	8.2
Services	55.9	55.8	56.1	56.0	56.9	58.0
C. Productivity growth[3]						
Agriculture	6.6	5.0	−1.0	11.0	8.4	5.1
Industry	3.6	2.4	0.3	−1.1	3.3	2.0
Construction	2.9	−0.1	2.2	8.2	−6.1	1.8
Services	0.5	0.0	−0.8	0.0	0.3	2.6
D. Sectoral distribution of foreign direct						
investment projects						
Manufacturing and mining	58.2	36.9	42.0	35.0	31.7	51.7
Trade and tourism	16.5	12.4	14.5	9.5	12.9	17.9
Financial sector	19.4	43.3	37.3	46.5	46.0	27.4
Other	5.9	7.4	6.3	9.0	9.4	3.1
E. Sectoral distribution of industrial employment						
Basic metals	3.0	2.6	2.4	2.2	2.2	2.3
Non-metallic minerals	6.4	6.2	6.4	6.6	6.5	6.8
Chemicals	6.3	5.5	6.0	6.0	5.8	5.1
Metal products	11.1	12.1	12.3	11.8	12.2	13.0
Electrical machinery	8.2	8.3	8.4	9.1	8.8	8.7
Electronic machinery and equipment	2.7	2.9	3.1	3.2	3.2	3.1
Automobiles	5.6	6.1	6.1	6.4	6.6	7.1
Other transport equipment	4.0	3.4	3.2	2.9	2.6	2.8
Food, beverages and tobacco	14.8	15.0	14.9	14.7	14.4	14.3
Textiles and clothing	18.6	18.3	17.1	16.9	16.8	15.7
Other	19.3	19.6	20.1	20.0	20.9	21.2

1. Annual average.
2. Provisional data.
3. Sectoral production/sectoral employment.
Source: Ministry of Labour and Social Affairs, *Boletín de Estadísticas Laborales* (1993), Bank of Spain, *Cuentas financieras* (1993), National Institute of Statistics, *Contabilidad Nacional* (1994) and Ministry of Economy and Finance.

BASIC STATISTICS:

INTERNATIONAL COMPARISONS

	Units	Reference period [1]	Australia	Austri
Population				
Total	Thousands	1991	17 292	7 823
Inhabitants per sq. km	Number	1991	2	93
Net average annual increase over previous 10 years	%	1991	1.5	0.3
Employment				
Total civilian employment (TCE) [2]	Thousands	1991	7 705	3 482
Of which: Agriculture	% of TCE		5.5	7.4
Industry	% of TCE		24.2	36.9
Services	% of TCE		70.4	55.8
Gross domestic product (GDP)				
At current prices and current exchange rates	Bill. US$	1991	297.4	164.7
Per capita	US$		17 200	21 048
At current prices using current PPP's [3]	Bill. US$	1991	280	135.6
Per capita	US$		16 195	17 329
Average annual volume growth over previous 5 years	%	1991	2.8	3.3
Gross fixed capital formation (GFCF)	% of GDP	1991	20.5	25.1
Of which: Machinery and equipment	% of GDP		8.8	10.4
Residential construction	% of GDP		4.6	4.6
Average annual volume growth over previous 5 years	%	1991	0.3	5.2
Gross saving ratio [4]	% of GDP	1991	17.2	25.6
General government				
Current expenditure on goods and services	% of GDP	1991	18.3	18.2
Current disbursements [5]	% of GDP	1991	36.6	45.7
Current receipts	% of GDP	1991	33.7	47.2
Net official development assistance	% of GDP	1991	0.35	0.33
Indicators of living standards				
Private consumption per capita using current PPP's [3]	US$	1991	9 827	9 591
Passenger cars, per 1 000 inhabitants	Number	1990	430	382
Telephones, per 1 000 inhabitants	Number	1990	448 (89)	589
Television sets, per 1 000 inhabitants	Number	1989	484	475
Doctors, per 1 000 inhabitants	Number	1991	2	2.1
Infant mortality per 1 000 live births	Number	1991	7.1	7.4
Wages and prices (average annual increase over previous 5 years)				
Wages (earnings or rates according to availability)	%	1991	5.4	5.2
Consumer prices	%	1991	6.7	2.5
Foreign trade				
Exports of goods, fob*	Mill. US$	1991	39 764	40 985
As % of GDP	%		13.4	24.9
Average annual increase over previous 5 years	%		13.2	12.8
Imports of goods, cif*	Mill. US$	1991	38 844	48 914
As % of GDP	%		13.1	29.7
Average annual increase over previous 5 years	%		10.1	13.7
Total official reserves [6]	Mill. SDR's	1991	11 432	6 591
As ratio of average monthly imports of goods	Ratio		3.5	1.6

* At current prices and exchange rates.
1. Unless otherwise stated.
2. According to the definitions used in OECD *Labour Force Statistics*.
3. PPP's = Purchasing Power Parities.
4. Gross saving = Gross national disposable income minus private and government consumption.
5. Current disbursements = Current expenditure on goods and services plus current transfers and payments of property income.
6. Gold included in reserves is valued at 35 SDR's per ounce. End of year.
7. Including Luxembourg.

Belgium	Spain	Sweden	Switzerland	Turkey	United Kingdom	United States
0 005	39 025	8 617	6 792	57 693	57 649	252 160
328	77	19	165	74	236	27
0.2	0.3	0.3	0.6	2.3	0.2	0.9
3 735	12 608	4 431	3 560	18 171	25 726	116 877
2.6	10.7	3.2	5.5	46.6	2.2	2.9
28.1	33.1	28.2	34.4	20.3	27.8	25.3
69.3	56.3	68.5	60.1	33.1	70	71.8
196.9	527.6	239.3	230.9	108	1 008.4	5 610.8
9 677	13 519	27 774	33 992	1 872	17 492	22 204
171.5	496.2	145.4	148.3	201.1	899.8	5 610.8
7 145	12 714	16 877	21 832	3 486	15 608	22 204
3.2	4.3	1.6	2.2	4.7	2	1.9
19.8	23.9	19.4	25.6	22.8	16.9	15.4
10.4 (	7.1					
4.2)	4.7	6.2	16.9[9]	5.8 (87)	3	3.4
8.5	9.9	3.3	4	3.1	2.8	−0.5
21.4	21	16	31.6	21.2	13.5	15
14.7	16.1	27.2	13.9	22.5	21.7	18.2
54.6)	35.5 (88)	59.8	32.5	..	39.7	36.7
49.8)	36.3 (88)	60	34.2	..	38.8	32.5
0.42	0.22	0.88	0.37	..	0.32	0.2
0 756	7 935	8 994	12 607	1995	9 912	14 891
387	307	418	441	29	361	568
546	323	681	905	151	434	509
447	389	471	406	174	434	814
3.6	3.9	2.9	3	0.9	1.4	2.3
8.4	7.8	6.1	6.2	56.5	7.4	8.9
3.5	7.6	7.7	..	..	8.6	2.8
2.5	5.9	7.2	3.5	60.3	6.4	4.4
8 291[7]	55 353	57 422	63 893	13 057	184 087	393 812
60.1	10.5	24	27.7	12.1	18.3	7
11.4	17.1	8.1	10.2	12.9	11.5	13.2
0 330[7]	87 449	54 659	69 863	22 566	222 522	494 842
61.1	16.6	22.8	30.3	20.9	22.1	8.8
12	21.6	8.8	10	13.5	10.7	6
8 541[7]	36 008	12 644	20 541	4 252	25 201	50 791
0.9	4.9	2.8	3.5	2.3	1.4	1.2

January, 1994

EMPLOYMENT OPPORTUNITIES

Economics Department, OECD

The Economics Department of the OECD offers challenging and rewarding opportunities to economists interested in applied policy analysis in an international environment. The Department's concerns extend across the entire field of economic policy analysis, both macro-economic and micro-economic. Its main task is to provide, for discussion by committees of senior officials from Member countries, documents and papers dealing with current policy concerns. Within this programme of work, three major responsibilities are:

- to prepare regular surveys of the economies of individual Member countries;
- to issue full twice-yearly reviews of the economic situation and prospects of the OECD countries in the context of world economic trends;
- to analyse specific policy issues in a medium-term context for theOECD as a whole, and to a lesser extent for the non-OECD countries.

The documents prepared for these purposes, together with much of the Department's other economic work, appear in published form in the *OECD Economic Outlook, OECD Economic Surveys, OECD Economic Studies* and the Department's *Working Papers* series.

The Department maintains a world econometric model, INTERLINK, which plays an important role in the preparation of the policy analyses and twice-yearly projections. The availability of extensive cross-country data bases and good computer resources facilitates comparative empirical analysis, much of which is incorporated into the model.

The Department is made up of about 75 professional economists from a variety of backgrounds and Member countries. Most projects are carried out by small teams and last from four to eighteen months. Within the Department, ideas and points of view are widely discussed; there is a lively professional interchange, and all professional staff have the opportunity to contribute actively to the programme of work.

Skills the Economics Department is looking for:

a) Solid competence in using the tools of both micro-economic and macro-economic theory to answer policy questions. Experience indicates that this normally requires the equivalent of a PH.D. in economics or substantial relevant professional experience to compensate for a lower degree.

b) Solid knowledge of economic statistics and quantitative methods; this includes how to identify data, estimate structural relationships, apply basic techniques of time series analysis, and test hypotheses. It is essential to be able to interpret results sensibly in an economic policy context.

c) A keen interest in and knowledge of policy issues, economic developments and their political/social contexts.
d) Interest and experience in analysing questions posed by policy-makers and presenting the results to them effectively and judiciously. Thus, work experience in government agencies or policy research institutions is an advantage.
e) The ability to write clearly, effectively, and to the point. The OECD is a bilingual organisation with French and English as the official languages. Candidates must have excellent knowledge of one of these languages, and some knowledge of the other. Knowledge of other languages might also be an advantage for certain posts.
f) For some posts, expertise in a particular area may be important, but a successful candidate is expected to be able to work on a broader range of topics relevant to the work of the Department. Thus, except in rare cases, the Department does not recruit narrow specialists.
g) The Department works on a tight time schedule and strict deadlines. Moreover, much of the work in the Department is carried out in small groups of economists. Thus, the ability to work with other economists from a variety of cultural and professional backgrounds, to supervise junior staff, and to produce work on time is important.

General Information

The salary for recruits depends on educational and professional background. Positions carry a basic salary from FF 262 512 or FF 323 916 for Administrators (economists) and from FF 375 708 for Principal Administrators (senior economists). This may be supplemented by expatriation and/or family allowances, depending on nationality, residence and family situation. Initial appointments are for a fixed term of two to three years.

Vacancies are open to candidates from OECD Member countries. The Organisation seeks to maintain an appropriate balance between female and male staff and among nationals from Member countries.

For further information on employment opportunities in the Economics Department, contact:

Administrative Unit
Economics Department
OECD
2, rue André-Pascal
75775 PARIS CEDEX 16
FRANCE

Applications citing "ECSUR", together with a detailed *curriculum vitae* in English or French, should be sent to the Head of Personnel at the above address.

MAIN SALES OUTLETS OF OECD PUBLICATIONS
PRINCIPAUX POINTS DE VENTE DES PUBLICATIONS DE L'OCDE

ARGENTINA – ARGENTINE
Carlos Hirsch S.R.L.
Galería Güemes, Florida 165, 4° Piso
1333 Buenos Aires   Tel. (1) 331.1787 y 331.2391
Telefax: (1) 331.1787

AUSTRALIA – AUSTRALIE
D.A. Information Services
648 Whitehorse Road, P.O.B 163
Mitcham, Victoria 3132   Tel. (03) 873.4411
Telefax: (03) 873.5679

AUSTRIA – AUTRICHE
Gerold & Co.
Graben 31
Wien I   Tel. (0222) 533.50.14

BELGIUM – BELGIQUE
Jean De Lannoy
Avenue du Roi 202
B-1060 Bruxelles   Tel. (02) 538.51.69/538.08.41
Telefax: (02) 538.08.41

CANADA
Renouf Publishing Company Ltd.
1294 Algoma Road
Ottawa, ON K1B 3W8   Tel. (613) 741.4333
Telefax: (613) 741.5439
Stores:
61 Sparks Street
Ottawa, ON K1P 5R1   Tel. (613) 238.8985
211 Yonge Street
Toronto, ON M5B 1M4   Tel. (416) 363.3171
Telefax: (416)363.59.63

Les Éditions La Liberté Inc.
3020 Chemin Sainte-Foy
Sainte-Foy, PQ G1X 3V6   Tel. (418) 658.3763
Telefax: (418) 658.3763

Federal Publications Inc.
165 University Avenue, Suite 701
Toronto, ON M5H 3B8   Tel. (416) 860.1611
Telefax: (416) 860.1608

Les Publications Fédérales
1185 Université
Montréal, QC H3B 3A7   Tel. (514) 954.1633
Telefax : (514) 954.1635

CHINA – CHINE
China National Publications Import
Export Corporation (CNPIEC)
16 Gongti E. Road, Chaoyang District
P.O. Box 88 or 50
Beijing 100704 PR   Tel. (01) 506.6688
Telefax: (01) 506.3101

DENMARK – DANEMARK
Munksgaard Book and Subscription Service
35, Nørre Søgade, P.O. Box 2148
DK-1016 København K   Tel. (33) 12.85.70
Telefax: (33) 12.93.87

FINLAND – FINLANDE
Akateeminen Kirjakauppa
Keskuskatu 1, P.O. Box 128
00100 Helsinki

Subscription Services/Agence d'abonnements :
P.O. Box 23
00371 Helsinki   Tel. (358 0) 12141
Telefax: (358 0) 121.4450

FRANCE
OECD/OCDE
Mail Orders/Commandes par correspondance:
2, rue André-Pascal
75775 Paris Cedex 16   Tel. (33-1) 45.24.82.00
Telefax: (33-1) 49.10.42.76
Telex: 640048 OCDE

OECD Bookshop/Librairie de l'OCDE :
33, rue Octave-Feuillet
75016 Paris   Tel. (33-1) 45.24.81.67
(33-1) 45.24.81.81

Documentation Française
29, quai Voltaire
75007 Paris   Tel. 40.15.70.00

Gibert Jeune (Droit-Économie)
6, place Saint-Michel
75006 Paris   Tel. 43.25.91.19

Librairie du Commerce International
10, avenue d'Iéna
75016 Paris   Tel. 40.73.34.60

Librairie Dunod
Université Paris-Dauphine
Place du Maréchal de Lattre de Tassigny
75016 Paris   Tel. (1) 44.05.40.13

Librairie Lavoisier
11, rue Lavoisier
75008 Paris   Tel. 42.65.39.95

Librairie L.G.D.J. - Montchrestien
20, rue Soufflot
75005 Paris   Tel. 46.33.89.85

Librairie des Sciences Politiques
30, rue Saint-Guillaume
75007 Paris   Tel. 45.48.36.02

P.U.F.
49, boulevard Saint-Michel
75005 Paris   Tel. 43.25.83.40

Librairie de l'Université
12a, rue Nazareth
13100 Aix-en-Provence   Tel. (16) 42.26.18.08

Documentation Française
165, rue Garibaldi
69003 Lyon   Tel. (16) 78.63.32.23

Librairie Decitre
29, place Bellecour
69002 Lyon   Tel. (16) 72.40.54.54

GERMANY – ALLEMAGNE
OECD Publications and Information Centre
August-Bebel-Allee 6
D-53175 Bonn 2   Tel. (0228) 959.120
Telefax: (0228) 959.12.17

GREECE – GRÈCE
Librairie Kauffmann
Mavrokordatou 9
106 78 Athens   Tel. (01) 32.55.321
Telefax: (01) 36.33.967

HONG-KONG
Swindon Book Co. Ltd.
13–15 Lock Road
Kowloon, Hong Kong   Tel. 366.80.31
Telefax: 739.49.75

HUNGARY – HONGRIE
Euro Info Service
POB 1271
1464 Budapest   Tel. (1) 111.62.16
Telefax : (1) 111.60.61

ICELAND – ISLANDE
Mál Mog Menning
Laugavegi 18, Pósthólf 392
121 Reykjavik   Tel. 162.35.23

INDIA – INDE
Oxford Book and Stationery Co.
Scindia House
New Delhi 110001   Tel.(11) 331.5896/5308
Telefax: (11) 332.5993
17 Park Street
Calcutta 700016   Tel. 240832

INDONESIA – INDONÉSIE
Pdii-Lipi
P.O. Box 269/JKSMG/88
Jakarta 12790   Tel. 583467
Telex: 62 875

IRELAND – IRLANDE
TDC Publishers – Library Suppliers
12 North Frederick Street
Dublin 1   Tel. (01) 874.48.35
Telefax: (01) 874.84.16

ISRAEL
Electronic Publications only
Publications électroniques seulement
Praedicta
5 Shatna Street
P.O. Box 34030
Jerusalem 91340   Tel. (2) 52.84.90/1/2
Telefax: (2) 52.84.93

ITALY – ITALIE
Libreria Commissionaria Sansoni
Via Duca di Calabria 1/1
50125 Firenze   Tel. (055) 64.54.15
Telefax: (055) 64.12.57
Via Bartolini 29
20155 Milano   Tel. (02) 36.50.83

Editrice e Libreria Herder
Piazza Montecitorio 120
00186 Roma   Tel. 679.46.28
Telefax: 678.47.51

Libreria Hoepli
Via Hoepli 5
20121 Milano   Tel. (02) 86.54.46
Telefax: (02) 805.28.86

Libreria Scientifica
Dott. Lucio de Biasio 'Aeiou'
Via Coronelli, 6
20146 Milano   Tel. (02) 48.95.45.52
Telefax: (02) 48.95.45.48

JAPAN – JAPON
OECD Publications and Information Centre
Landic Akasaka Building
2-3-4 Akasaka, Minato-ku
Tokyo 107   Tel. (81.3) 3586.2016
Telefax: (81.3) 3584.7929

KOREA – CORÉE
Kyobo Book Centre Co. Ltd.
P.O. Box 1658, Kwang Hwa Moon
Seoul   Tel. 730.78.91
Telefax: 735.00.30

MALAYSIA – MALAISIE
Co-operative Bookshop Ltd.
University of Malaya
P.O. Box 1127, Jalan Pantai Baru
59700 Kuala Lumpur
Malaysia   Tel. 756.5000/756.5425
Telefax: 757.3661

MEXICO – MEXIQUE
Revistas y Periodicos Internacionales S.A. de C.V.
Florencia 57 - 1004
Mexico, D.F. 06600   Tel. 207.81.00
Telefax : 208.39.79

NETHERLANDS – PAYS-BAS
SDU Uitgeverij Plantijnstraat
Externe Fondsen
Postbus 20014
2500 EA 's-Gravenhage   Tel. (070) 37.89.880
Voor bestellingen: Telefax: (070) 34.75.778

**NEW ZEALAND
NOUVELLE-ZÉLANDE**
Legislation Services
P.O. Box 12418
Thorndon, Wellington   Tel. (04) 496.5652
   Telefax: (04) 496.5698

NORWAY – NORVÈGE
Narvesen Info Center – NIC
Bertrand Narvesens vei 2
P.O. Box 6125 Etterstad
0602 Oslo 6   Tel. (022) 57.33.00
   Telefax: (022) 68.19.01

PAKISTAN
Mirza Book Agency
65 Shahrah Quaid-E-Azam
Lahore 54000   Tel. (42) 353.601
   Telefax: (42) 231.730

PHILIPPINE – PHILIPPINES
International Book Center
5th Floor, Filipinas Life Bldg.
Ayala Avenue
Metro Manila   Tel. 81.96.76
   Telex 23312 RHP PH

PORTUGAL
Livraria Portugal
Rua do Carmo 70-74
Apart. 2681
1200 Lisboa   Tel.: (01) 347.49.82/5
   Telefax: (01) 347.02.64

SINGAPORE – SINGAPOUR
Gower Asia Pacific Pte Ltd.
Golden Wheel Building
41, Kallang Pudding Road, No. 04-03
Singapore 1334   Tel. 741.5166
   Telefax: 742.9356

SPAIN – ESPAGNE
Mundi-Prensa Libros S.A.
Castelló 37, Apartado 1223
Madrid 28001   Tel. (91) 431.33.99
   Telefax: (91) 575.39.98

Libreria Internacional AEDOS
Consejo de Ciento 391
08009 – Barcelona   Tel. (93) 488.30.09
   Telefax: (93) 487.76.59

Llibreria de la Generalitat
Palau Moja
Rambla dels Estudis, 118
08002 – Barcelona
   (Subscripcions) Tel. (93) 318.80.12
   (Publicacions) Tel. (93) 302.67.23
   Telefax: (93) 412.18.54

SRI LANKA
Centre for Policy Research
c/o Colombo Agencies Ltd.
No. 300-304, Galle Road
Colombo 3   Tel. (1) 574240, 573551-2
   Telefax: (1) 575394, 510711

SWEDEN – SUÈDE
Fritzes Information Center
Box 16356
Regeringsgatan 12
106 47 Stockholm   Tel. (08) 690.90.90
   Telefax: (08) 20.50.21

Subscription Agency/Agence d'abonnements :
Wennergren-Williams Info AB
P.O. Box 1305
171 25 Solna   Tel. (08) 705.97.50
   Téléfax : (08) 27.00.71

SWITZERLAND – SUISSE
Maditec S.A. (Books and Periodicals - Livres
et périodiques)
Chemin des Palettes 4
Case postale 266
1020 Renens   Tel. (021) 635.08.65
   Telefax: (021) 635.07.80

Librairie Payot S.A.
4, place Pépinet
CP 3212
1002 Lausanne   Tel. (021) 341.33.48
   Telefax: (021) 341.33.45

Librairie Unilivres
6, rue de Candolle
1205 Genève   Tel. (022) 320.26.23
   Telefax: (022) 329.73.18

Subscription Agency/Agence d'abonnements :
Dynapresse Marketing S.A.
38 avenue Vibert
1227 Carouge   Tel.: (022) 308.07.89
   Telefax : (022) 308.07.99

See also – Voir aussi :
OECD Publications and Information Centre
August-Bebel-Allee 6
D-53175 Bonn 2 (Germany)   Tel. (0228) 959.120
   Telefax: (0228) 959.12.17

TAIWAN – FORMOSE
Good Faith Worldwide Int'l. Co. Ltd.
9th Floor, No. 118, Sec. 2
Chung Hsiao E. Road
Taipei   Tel. (02) 391.7396/391.7397
   Telefax: (02) 394.9176

THAILAND – THAÏLANDE
Suksit Siam Co. Ltd.
113, 115 Fuang Nakhon Rd.
Opp. Wat Rajbopith
Bangkok 10200   Tel. (662) 225.9531/2
   Telefax: (662) 222.5188

TURKEY – TURQUIE
Kültür Yayinlari Is-Türk Ltd. Sti.
Atatürk Bulvari No. 191/Kat 13
Kavaklidere/Ankara   Tel. 428.11.40 Ext. 2458
Dolmabahce Cad. No. 29
Besiktas/Istanbul   Tel. 260.71.88
   Telex: 43482B

UNITED KINGDOM – ROYAUME-UNI
HMSO
Gen. enquiries   Tel. (071) 873 0011
Postal orders only:
P.O. Box 276, London SW8 5DT
Personal Callers HMSO Bookshop
49 High Holborn, London WC1V 6HB
   Telefax: (071) 873 8200
Branches at: Belfast, Birmingham, Bristol, Edin-
burgh, Manchester

UNITED STATES – ÉTATS-UNIS
OECD Publications and Information Centre
2001 L Street N.W., Suite 700
Washington, D.C. 20036-4910 Tel. (202) 785.6323
   Telefax: (202) 785.0350

VENEZUELA
Libreria del Este
Avda F. Miranda 52, Aptdo. 60337
Edificio Galipán
Caracas 106   Tel. 951.1705/951.2307/951.1297
   Telegram: Libreste Caracas

Subscription to OECD periodicals may also be
placed through main subscription agencies.

Les abonnements aux publications périodiques de
l'OCDE peuvent être souscrits auprès des
principales agences d'abonnement.

Orders and inquiries from countries where Distributors have not yet been appointed should be sent to:
OECD Publications Service, 2 rue André-Pascal,
75775 Paris Cedex 16, France.

Les commandes provenant de pays où l'OCDE n'a
pas encore désigné de distributeur devraient être
adressées à : OCDE, Service des Publications,
2, rue André-Pascal, 75775 Paris Cedex 16, France.

3-1994

PRINTED IN FRANCE

•

**OECD PUBLICATIONS
2 rue André-Pascal
75775 PARIS CEDEX 16
No. 47293
(10 94 24 1) ISBN 92-64-14155-3
ISSN 0376-6438**

•